S0-EMF-241

POPULAR SCIENCE

DO-IT-YOURSELF

ENCYCLOPEDIA

POPULAR SCIENCE

DO-IT-YOURSELF

ENCYCLOPEDIA

. . . Complete How-To *Series for the Entire Family . . .*

•

written in simple language

•

with full step-by-step instructions

•

and profusely illustrated

ILLUSTRATED EDITION

Volume 9

Out - Plu

ACKNOWLEDGMENTS

The editors of this series would like to express their thanks and appreciation to the following companies for their assistance in preparing special sections within this volume, for their technical advice and their permission to use special material, photographs, art and educational charts.

ALSYNITE COMPANY OF AMERICA   ARMSTRONG CORK CO.   BAKER BRUSH CO.   DIAMOND CALK HORSHOE CO.   DOUGLAS FIR PLYWOOD ASSOCIATION   E Z PAINTR CORP.   FILON CO.   THE FORMICA COMPANY   KRAFTILE CO.   MANOR CRAFTS CO.   MASONITE CORP.   MONSANTO CHEMICAL CO.   NATIONAL COTTON COUNCIL   NATIONAL PAINT, VARNISH AND LACQUER ASSOCIATION   OWENS-CORNING FIBERGLAS CORP.   PITTSBURGH PLATE GLASS CO.   PLASTI-KOTE, INC.   PREPO CORP.   RED DEVIL TOOLS, INC.   SAKRETE, INC.   REYNOLDS METALS CO.   W. L. SIMS   STANLEY TOOLS, DIVISION OF THE STANLEY WORKS   TILEMASTER CORP.   UNITED STATES PLYWOOD CORP.   UNITED STATES RUBBER CO.   VALSPAR CO.   WASHINGTON STEEL PRODUCTS, INC.   WAYNE PRODUCTS CO.   WEN PRODUCTS   WILSON IMPERIAL CO.

Outdoor Lighting Projects

An old porch post salvaged from a junk yard makes a handsome support for a yard lamp. The square block originally on top of this one was sawed off and the diameter reduced enough to suit the lamp chosen. To add height, a 36" piece of timber square to match was added to the bottom of the post, a splint-type joint being used. After a slot ¾" deep had been cut up one side, the cable was wedged in, and the slot puttied full with water-mix filler. Paint, applied after the post was erected, hid the slot. Use enough lead or vinyl cable to reach from the house to the lamp without splicing.

MAKING A LAMPPOST AND AN OUTLET

1. Tall lamp at right begins with four 8′ lengths of 1x4's. Nail two of them together. Mount a standard switch box inside, as shown here, about 24″ from the bottom end of one of the boards.

Nail on third side—Cut a square piece to fit top and mount a socket on it, drilling two small holes to bring wires through. Run wires from socket to box, leaving about 5″ of extra wire for connections.

Notch fourth board to fit around the electric box. Then complete the lamppost as shown in the photograph and fasten the square bearing the socket securely to the top of the post with four screws.

2. Weatherproof outlet goes in the box. Connect to both socket and wires coming in from bottom. The latter will ordinarily be trench cable running to a source of power at the house.

3. Bracket for shade consists of four 14" length of 1x2's, rounded off. Fasten each to post with only one screw to begin with. Then make a cylindrical plastic shade as seen on the facing page.

4. Adjust brackets to fit shade and screw them to post. Use rust-proof screws to fasten shade to brackets, and secure a pie plate to bracket tops. Plate reflects light, and protects socket from rain.

5. Setting post in concrete will give it long-lasting rigidity. This can be done as shown in sketch. Before setting, be sure to coat bottom of post with wood preservative. Completed, you have a source of power in yard, as well as a lamp.

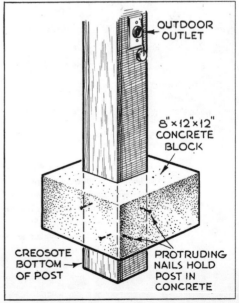

OUTDOOR OUTLET

8"×12"×12" CONCRETE BLOCK

CREOSOTE BOTTOM OF POST

PROTRUDING NAILS HOLD POST IN CONCRETE

Colonial Lights

With street lighting sketchy at best, the colonial home needed gate and porch lamps to light both visitor and homecomer. Today's porch light is a matter of course, but its styling need not be.

If your vacation takes you to Williamsburg, Jamestown, Charlottesville or other historic spots, you'll see many types of house lanterns worth copying. The originals were of course handmade, so they are naturals for the craftsman to duplicate.

You can build good-looking replicas of such antique lamps from tin-can stock, wire and glass. Standard electric fittings bring them up to date, making them as useful as they are ornamental.

Seen on a house in colonial Williamsburg, the original of this lantern came from a collection. The homemade version above is soldered up of tin-can-stock, coat-hanger wire and an old chandelier fitting. Glass panes should be the frosted kind if bulb is in line of sight. The wall lamp above is an electrified copy of one on the same house. Its bright tin-plate reflector throws plenty of light. Dull black, bronze or gold stippled on black are all suitable finishes.

 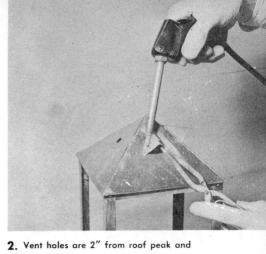

1. Cut tin-can stock into 1" strips. Bend them up to make ½"x½" angles. Solder together two 6¼"x7" frames, and join them with 6¼" pieces, to form the body.

2. Vent holes are 2" from roof peak and in the center of each side. Hoods to keep rain out are small triangles of tin plate, folded in middle and soldered over holes.

HOW TO MAKE A SQUARE LANTERN

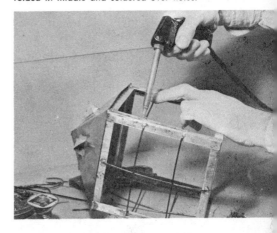

3. To shield glass and further the colonial effect, solder on guards made of coathanger wire. File each end bright, hammer flat and use acid flux to solder. Wash all joints well.

4. Base is removable for changing bulb. Make it of twice-folded tin plate. Solder short screws (arrow) into the frame. Drill holes in base. Retain with knurled nuts.

5. Ring fixture, from an old chandelier, screws onto ⅛" brass pipe soldered into roof. Cord passes down a corner. Insert panes from bottom and solder in clips.

MAKING A LIGHT DIFFUSER

1. Frame for picnic-table light diffuser is a 34"x34" assembly of 2x2's (actually about 1¾" square). Corner braces, cut off at 45° angle, measure 13" on long sides. Assemble with waterproof glue and rust-resistant hardware. Finish with spar varnish.

2. For octagonal diffuser, use a 26" square of yellow or rose-colored structural plastic. (This material is most readily available in 26" widths.) Measure 7⅜" both ways from each corner, scratch a line between connecting points and cut off the corners.

3. Plastic is secured to frame with plastic clothesline. Drill ¼" holes around plastic and frame; lace in the plastic. Hang the diffuser with more line. Use a plain bulb in a weatherproof socket or— better yet— a weatherproof bulb-socket combination.

Packaging Efficiency

For purposes of storing or sending parcels, here are a few good ideas to assist you:

Labeling for Storage—Put a label on every package which you put away in the attic or cedar closet or basement, to indicate what is inside that box or package. Then, when you open up the package, you will save time and energy by identifying the contents at once.

Labeling for Mailing—If you make a package to be sent by mail or messenger, and want to be sure that the address you wrote will not become blurred through handling or bad weather, put a strip of transparent cellophane tape over your writing. Or, if you don't have such cellophane tape, you can take a white candle and rub the bottom of it over your writing; this acts as a protective coating.

Tying a Package—Tying with a damp cord is a unique way to make a strong package. Wet the cord or twine (but not excessively so it will soak through the wrapping) before you use it to tie the package. The cord shrinks as it dries on the package, and this, of course, makes the knot much tighter.

Packing

Special impregnated cord is used to prevent leaking at valve joints in plumbing lines; this cord is referred to as packing. See *Faucet* and *Valves*.

Handle Screw
Handle
Cap Nut
Cone Bonnet Packing
Top Bibb Washer
Stem

Paint Remover

To remove paint from any surface, you have a choice of four different methods; you can use:

1. sandpaper, either by hand or with a powered sander
2. heat, with a blowtorch or an electric paint remover
3. special scrapers designed to "plane" the layers of paint off the surfaces
4. a chemical paint remover.

Using Chemical Removers

There are many different chemical paint removers available. Some come in powdered form and have to be mixed, others come in pres-

Chemical paint removers should be laid on wtih the flat side of the brush. Unlike paint, it should not be "worked out" or spread over the surface. Furthermore, do not go over an area once the remover has been applied, unless another coat is needed.

Photographs courtesy of Wilson Imperial Co.

Once the chemical remover has loosened the paint film, use a putty knife or scraper to peel off the old paint layers down to the bare wood.

A blowtorch can be used to remove old paint from any type of a surface. Keep the torch far enough away from the surface so as not to cause the paint to burn but close enough to soften it. Once it is softened, use a putty knife to scrape off the old paint.

Photograph courtesy of Prepo Corp.

Hand sanding is another way of removing paint from a surface. However, a surface with many layers of paint on it would require an extensive amount of sandpaper and a great deal of time to clean to the bare wood. Sanding is often necessary after the paint has been removed by other methods to make the surface smooth.

Photograph courtesy of Monsanto Chemical Co.

surized aerosol cans and others come in liquid form, ready-mixed, under various trade names such as Wonder-Paste.

To use the liquid chemical removers, you need a full-haired brush, a 2″ scraping knife, a bucket for the remover, steel wool, dropcloths, wire brush, cloths, alcohol for washing the surface after the paint has been scraped off.

The paint remover is applied with a brush, laying it on with the flat side of the brush, in one direction only (as shown in the accompanying photograph). Give it a good full coat for you should not go back and brush over it again. Con-

tinue to apply the remover over the remainder of the area, covering as much as you can in twenty minutes.

Once the twenty minutes are up, go back to where you started with a scraping knife. Test to see if the film has softened all the way down to the wood. If it has, go ahead and scrape off the paint layer. If the film has not softened all the way down to the wood, recoat the area again in the same manner as you did before.

Unless the finish is very old, two coats and one hour of time will be sufficient to soften the whole paint

A power sander is sometimes used to remove old paint prior to refinishing. This is a good technique on small pieces and where there are only a few layers of paint to be removed. It is also recommended on surfaces which might be adversely affected by the chemical pain removers, such as home inlaid and veneered work.

Photograph courtesy of Wen Products.

film. Don't rush the remover. Let it do all the hard work! If more time is needed, allow it! On extremely heavily coated surfaces, a third coat of the remover may be necessary.

After you have scraped the paint from the surface, wash with cloths saturated with alcohol. When using removers, it generally will not be necessary to sand the surface since the remover does not raise the grain. However, check the grain by hand; if it's raised, then sand with fine sandpaper until smooth.

Using a Blowtorch

Extreme care is necessary when working with a blowtorch to remove paint to make certain that you do not violate safety rules concerning fire. Do not work near open windows and flying curtains; make certain that there is nothing inflammable about. When removing paint from around a window, keep the torch moving and avoid playing the flame on the glass—it's likely to crack it.

It is best to keep the torch in motion all the time you are playing the flame on the painted surface. If the paint starts to burn, you are holding the torch too close. Hold the blowtorch close enough to heat the paint film, but not to start a fire.

Furthermore, by continually moving the torch, you will avoid the possibility of scorching the wood. If you are removing paint from metal, make certain not to touch any part, even where the torch did not heat it. The metal conducts heat and the entire piece may cause a burn or even start a fire if you are not careful.

See *Soldering* and *Torches*.

Using Sanders and Scrapers

There are many different types of scrapers that can be used to remove paint. Some are flat surfaces while others are made irregular in order to reach into grooves around moldings or trim.

Sanding requires care, especially when working with a powered sander. In using the latter, keep the sander moving at all times so that you do not "eat" into the wood and cause an uneven surface.

See *Abrasives* and *Sanders*.

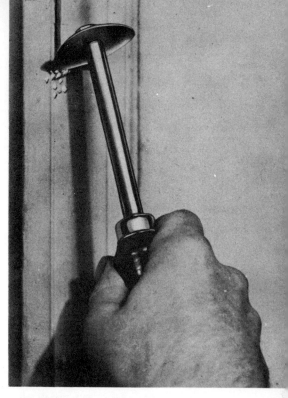

Scrapers come in many shapes, depending upon the job for which they are designed to do. This "Ogee" or "Half-Ogee" hand scraper is made to remove old paint from crevices and recesses, which cannot be reached with flat scrapers or putty knives.

Photograph courtesy of Red Devil Tools.

Painting

Amateur house painters never had as much help as today. Scores of new paints and equipment placed on the market in the last few years make it possible for the weekend handyman to paint his own house almost as easily as a professional. From one-coat paints to disposable blowtorches, everything has been designed to make the job go faster, look better and cost less.

With the new outside rollers, you can paint an average-size house in a couple of days. Add an extension handle and you can roll a terrace without stooping down, reach a roof without leaving the ground.

Paintbrush on a pole spreads paint on the high spots without special ladders or scaffolds, is one of many new tools that help amateurs do a professional job. Holder shown takes either brush or roller, fits on mop or broom handle and can be set at any angle to get in corners, crevices and under overhangs.

Painting Hard Spots

Badly rusted metal can be covered over with this new paint, saving work of cleaning metal first. Paint stops rust chemically, comes in several colors and can be used as finish coat or as undercoat for regular paint.

Specialized aids with built-in know-how tackle the hard spots for you.

Better still, you don't have to spend hours getting ready and hours cleaning up afterward. Premixed paints, electric-drill attachments and self-dispensing calking guns make short work of preparation. Cleaning up is a soap-and-water job for the rubber paints, or a quick dip in special cleaners for the oils. Disposable dropcloths and paper paint pails are used once and thrown away.

In this section are some tips on techniques and tools that make it easier to paint your house than ever before—not the way the "pro" does, perhaps, but with much the same results.

The term paint is used to include paints, varnishes, enamels, shellacs, lacquers, and stains.

• Paints are composed of mineral pigments, organic vehicles, and

Spray cans get in where brushes won't reach, provide easy way to paint screens, shutters, iron grillwork. Screens stacked this way can be sprayed three or four at a time to save paint. Spray screens from both sides.

a variety of thinners all combined.

• Varnishes are resins dissolved in organic thinners.

• Enamels are pigmented var--nishes.

• Shellac is lac gum dissolved in alcohol.

• Lacquers may be both pigmented or clear—the liquid portion usually is treated nitrocellulose dissolved in thinners.

• Stains may be pigmented oil or a penetrating type.

Many of these materials, such as paints, varnishes, and lacquers, are formulated for specific purposes:

• Outside house paints and exterior varnishes are intended to give good service when exposed to weathering.

• Interior wall paints are formulated to give excellent coverage and good washability.

• Floor enamels are made to withstand abrasion.

• Lacquers are formulated for rapid drying.

• There are also formulas which provide extra self-cleaning, fume-resisting, waterproofing, hardening, flexibility, mildew-resisting, resistance to fading, and breathing qualities.

Interior paints are used to obtain pleasing decorative effects, improve sanitary conditions, and insure better lighting. These paints may be divided into four types: wall primers; one-coat flats; flat, semigloss, and gloss; and water paints.

Wall primers or primer-sealers are intended to be applied directly to bare plaster, wallboard, and similar porous surfaces to provide a uniform, sealed surface for subsequent coats of paint. A typical wall primer may be made from varnish or bodied-oil vehicle and hiding pigments. It is intended to penetrate only slightly into porous surfaces.

Rubber-base masonry paint lets you put a quick coat on brick, stucco or cement without mixing up powders or using special undercoats. It comes ready to use, is waterproof, can also be used on asbestos shingles.

You can roll paint on a concrete porch or outdoor terrace with an extension handle and this rubber-base enamel. Enamel is tough, wears better than ordinary concrete paints, is not affected by moisture in exposed slabs.

The primers are best applied with a wide wall brush.

One-coat flat paints are organic-solvent-thinned paints intended to accomplish priming, sealing, and finish coating in one operation. They are often sold in thin paste form so that additional inexpensive thinner may be added and mixed before application to increase the volume of

WHICH PAINT TO USE . . . AND WHERE

Exterior Surfaces

Surface	HOUSE PAINT	WATER REPELLANT	CEMENT BASE PAINT	RUBBER-BASE PAINT	EMULSION PAINT (INCLUDING LATEX)(NO LATEX)	PENETRATING PAINT	ALUMINUM SEALER	WOOD STAIN	TRIM-AND-TRELLIS PAINT	AWNING PAINT	SPAR VARNISH	PORCH-AND-DECK PAINT	PRIMER OR UNDERCOATER	METAL PRIMER
WOOD SIDING (Painted)	✓•												✓	
WOOD SIDING (Natural)						✓		✓		✓				
BRICK	✓•	✓	✓	✓	✓								✓	
CEMENT & CINDER BLOCK	✓•	✓	✓	✓	✓								✓	
ASBESTOS CEMENT	✓•			✓	✓								✓	
STUCCO	✓•	✓	✓	✓	✓								✓	
STONE	✓•	✓	✓	✓	✓								✓	
ASPHALT SHINGLE SIDING	✓•			✓		✓								
METAL SIDING	✓•								✓•					✓
WOOD FRAME WINDOWS	✓•								✓•				✓	
STEEL WINDOWS	✓•								✓•					✓
ALUMINUM WINDOWS	✓•								✓•					✓
SHUTTERS & OTHER TRIM									✓•				✓	
CLOTH AWNINGS										✓				
WOOD SHINGLE ROOF								✓						
WOOD PORCH FLOOR												✓		
CEMENT PORCH FLOOR			✓									✓		
COPPER SURFACES											✓			
GALVANIZED SURFACES	✓•						✓•		✓•		✓			✓
IRON SURFACES	✓•						✓•		✓•					✓

✓• Black dot indicates that a primer or sealer may be necessary before the finishing coat (unless surface has been previously finished.)

paint by one-fourth or more.

Flat, semigloss, and gloss interior paints and enamels vary in degree of gloss, hiding power, and other properties. Paints giving the best hiding power are normally paints of lowest gloss, although some modern high-gloss enamels also have good hiding power.

Water-thinned interior paints are calcimine, casein, resin-emulsion, and gloss water paints. Calcimine consists of powdered whiting and clay mixed with an animal-glue binder and a preservative. It cannot be recoated, but can be easily washed off before redecorating. (For more information, see section on *Calcimine*).

It is not necessary to remove casein before recoating but, if desired, it can be softened by washing with hot solutions of trisodium phosphate. Resin-emulsion paints, marketed in paste form, are to be thinned with water and, when properly made and applied, adhere well to plaster and provide a good decorative medium. They need not be removed before redecorating, provided the film is in sound condition. This is also true of gloss water paints.

New Paints Give You Pro's Skill

Painting your house will be easier than ever—if you get the right paint. But it's going to be harder than ever to pick it.

Years ago, paint was paint. One kind looked, smelled, was applied and eventually dried much like an-

Getting Ready

Rough spots on old paint are quickly smoothed down with sanding wheel in electric drill. Same treatment with wire-brush wheel (in foreground) takes rust and scale off metalwork. Cracked and peeling paint can be removed with several types of hand scrapers.

Disposable blowtorch takes off heavily built-up or alligatored paint, needs no pumping or priming, is simply fitted with new tank when old one runs dry. Wide-mouth burner tip spreads flame over large area. Long-handled scraper keeps fingers out of way.

Calking gun fills cracks around windows, doors, needs no cleaning since barrel is disposable cartridge, replaced by refill. Calking compound can be painted over immediately.

V-shaped putty knife spreads smooth, professional bead of putty along window sash. Loose old putty should be removed and window primed before new putty is applied.

other. Things are different now. Besides oil paints, you can choose from a new set of paints. It'll pay you to know about them.

• There are water paints you can use outside. (You clean your brushes under the faucet and use the garden hose to get spatters off the shrubbery.)

• There are finishes so tough they withstand even attacks from the neighbors' children.

• There are paints that dry so fast you start the second coat as soon as you finish putting on the first.

• There are colors in glittering confusion.

No single product can do all these things. There are several types, all available under a variety of trade names. The trade names are, to put it kindly, confusing. For example, two brands of the new paints use "rubber" in their trade names, yet neither is a rubber-latex paint and each is actually an entirely different type of paint from the other. To get the right paint you have to read the fine print on the label and find out what is actually inside the can.

Vinyl is a cousin to the tough plastic used for upholstery and floor tiles, but it comes thinned with water ready for you to brush, roll or spray on. The label on the can may say vinyl, vinyl emulsion, polyvinyl acetate or PVA.

You can use vinyl on almost any exterior except previously painted wood. It works fine on wood shingles and shakes, asbestos shingles, brick, stucco, concrete and masonry blocks. One manufacturer says you can even put it on wood clapboard if the clapboard is new and unprimed.

The major advantage of vinyl is the thinner—water. You get all the advantages of easy cleanup that have made interior water paints so popular.

Extension ring fits top of paint can, making it easy to mix paint and add thinner without spilling. Ring has its own lid so it can be left on and paint kept covered. Ring can be used again with other paint.

Suppose it rains while you're working? Vinyl paint dries fast—as quickly as 10 to 30 minutes—and will withstand a shower after that time. It takes another 12 hours to "cure," by then forming an exceptionally tough, long-lasting film that stands up well against weather, sun, salt air and factory smoke.

One precaution: You can't paint with it in cold weather. The chemical reaction that transforms the water solution into a durable finish will not take place if the temperature is below 50°. (Conventional oil paints don't stick well in cold weather, either.)

Some manufacturers recommend their vinyl paints for interior as well as exterior use; others say no, not so good. There are vinyls made specifically for interiors.

Definitely good inside the house is a new vinyl primer-sealer to be used as a base coat under any paint. It dries in as little as 30 minutes.

You can put it around a room and probably follow immediately with the finish coat. It can be applied with brush or roller.

Acrylic is the second new name for magic in paints. This is also a plastic-in-water. Solid acrylic you know as the beautiful, glasslike Plexiglas and Lucite.

Inside the house is where acrylic shines. It dries faster than other types, and it keeps its color better, without yellowing. One disadvantage: It costs more.

Some acrylics are also recommended for exteriors (over the same kinds of materials as vinyl paints). Here it has a big advantage—you don't have to pick your painting weather so carefully. It can be applied on humid days and in cold seasons, so long as the temperature is a few degrees above freezing.

Alkyd is an old interior paint made newly popular by a change in solvent—a super-refined petroleum chemical that has almost no odor. It is not a water paint. You thin it and clean brushes with mineral spirits or turpentine, or, if you want to retain the odorless feature, with the new odorless solvent. (Ask the paint-store man for just that, odorless solvent.)

Alkyd has solid advantages overriding the slight cleanup inconvenience. It is exceptionally tough and very resistant to scrubbing. It stands up well in the trouble spots—trim, bathroom, kitchen. And it is easy to apply, producing a smooth, even finish free of streaks and brush marks.

The alkyds have little odor, but don't forget that the solvent is a petroleum product and its vapor is there even if you can't smell it. It can make you sick and it burns very easily, like the vapor of older paint solvents. So play safe: Keep windows open and keep flames away.

The old reliables are not to be overlooked either. Conventional *oil paints* can now be had in deodorized version, made with the same odor-less solvent used in the alkyds. And oil paint has much in its favor. It is sold everywhere; its virtues and faults are well established through centuries of use; it makes a tough film on almost any surface; it offers the greatest color range; and it is often cheaper.

Water-thinned   *rubber-latex* paint is already an old reliable,

WHICH PAINT TO USE . . . AND WHERE
Interior Surfaces

Surface	FLAT PAINT	SEMI-GLOSS PAINT	ENAMEL	RUBBER BASE PAINT	EMULSION PAINT (NOT LATEX)	CASEIN PAINT (INCLUDING LATEX)	INTERIOR VARNISH	SHELLAC	WAX (LIQUID OR PASTE)	WAX (EMULSION)	STAIN	WOOD SEALER	FLOOR VARNISH	FLOOR SEALER	CEMENT BASE PAINT OR ENAMEL	ALUMINUM PAINT	SEALER OR UNDERCOATER	METAL PRIMER
PLASTER WALLS & CEILING	●✓	●✓	✓	✓	✓												✓	
WALL BOARD	●✓	●✓	✓	✓	✓												✓	
WOOD PANELING	●✓	●✓	✓	●✓			✓	✓	✓		✓	✓						
KITCHEN & BATHROOM WALLS		●✓	●✓	✓	✓												✓	
WOOD FLOORS							✓	✓	●✓	●✓	✓	●✓	✓	●✓				
CONCRETE FLOORS									●✓	●✓	✓			✓	✓			
VINYL & RUBBER TILE FLOORS									✓	✓								
ASPHALT TILE FLOORS										✓								
LINOLEUM							✓	✓	✓			✓	✓					
STAIR TREADS									✓		✓	✓	✓	✓				
STAIR RISERS	●✓	●✓	●✓	✓			✓	✓			✓	✓						
WOOD TRIM	●✓	●✓	●✓	✓	●✓		✓	✓	✓		✓						✓	
STEEL WINDOWS	●✓	●✓	●✓	✓												✓		✓
ALUMINUM WINDOWS	●✓	●✓	●✓	✓												✓		✓
WINDOW SILLS			●✓			✓												
STEEL CABINETS	●✓	●✓	●✓	✓														✓
HEATING DUCTS	●✓	●✓	●✓	✓												✓		✓
RADIATORS & HEATING PIPES	●✓	●✓	●✓	✓												✓		✓
OLD MASONRY	✓	✓	✓	✓	✓	✓									✓	✓	✓	
NEW MASONRY	●✓	●✓	●✓	✓	✓										✓		✓	

●✓ Black dot indicates that a primer or sealer may be necessary before the finishing coat (unless surface has been previously finished.)

Applying the Paint

Exterior rollers now let you paint outside with the same ease as inside. Small doughnut-shaped roller (left) gets in corners, under edges of clapboards and between joints in vertical siding. Then large roller is used to fill in broad areas (right). Special long-nap roller also puts paint on brick, stucco and other rough-surface masonry. Paint tray clamps to side of ladder, can be adjusted to any angle.

Miniature roller lays narrow ribbon of paint on window sash without getting paint on glass. Roller comes with its own tiny paint tray, has metal tip that rides against glass to keep paint from smearing. Another type of sash painter (on window sill) has plush pad set in plastic handle. Pad is saturated with paint, then wiped along sash with plastic edge held against window to keep paint off glass.

Easel for painting screens and storm windows is made by clipping special wire hooks to stepladder rung. Hooks also serve as paintcan holders for working atop ladders.

You can stand on ground and still reach first-floor roof overhangs with roller on extension handle like this. You paint as fast as you walk, don't have to keep moving ladder. Same extension will reach second-floor overhangs from stepladder.

though it is only about 10 years old. It accounts for a big percentage of all paint sold and is still the most widely available of the easy-to-use finishes. One new type is a combination vinyl-rubber paint that is said to do a better job on interiors than either vinyl or rubber alone because it dries faster, lasts longer and has less sheen.

Trick ladder does several jobs in one. As stepladder, it stands 7', lets you reach well above first-floor line. By locking one half to other, it converts into 13' extension ladder, for reaching high spots. Halves can also be used separately as short ladders so two persons can paint at once.

Here's the Score on the New Paint	Emulsion Finishes				Solvent Finishes	
	RUBBER	VINYL	RUBBER-VINYL	ACRYLIC	ALKYD	OIL
Exterior	No*	Most	No	Some	No	Most
Interior	Yes	Some	Yes	Most	Yes	Some
Thin With	Water	Water (Unless can label specifies special reducer)	Water	Water	Mineral spirits, turpentine or odorless solvent if paint is odorless type	Mineral spirits, turpentine or odorless solvent if paint is odorless type
Clean Up With	Water	Water	Water	Water	Mineral spirits, turpentine or odorless solvent	Mineral spirits, turpentine or odorless solvent
Drying Time (Time between coats)	3–4 Hours	2 Hours	2 Hours	1–2 Hours	Overnight	Exterior: 2–3 Days Interior: 8 hours

*Generally not recommended for exterior use, but some special types are available for outdoor use.

Paint Selection

Most paints are purchased ready-mixed but, in their selection, consideration should be given to the fact that surfaces vary in their adaptability to paint and atmospheric or other conditions having an adverse effect on paint performance. In addition to the normal weathering action of sun and rain, outside house paints are sometimes exposed to other atacking elements, such as corrosive fumes from factories or excessive amounts of wind-driven dust.

For localities where such conditions exist, self-cleaning paints should be selected. These paints are usually so designated on the label. Concrete, plaster, and metal surfaces each present special problems in painting. For instance, paint for use on masonry or new plaster must be resistant to dampness and alkalies, and paints used on steel must have rust-inhibitive properties.

Color—The paint makers are out to sell the lady of the house and color is their come-on. They are tempting her with a kaleidoscope's variety; one firm offers more than 6,000 different shades.

Practically every manufacturer has a "color system," a fat book of color chips with instructions for duplicating each chip. This is accomplished by intermixing cans of colored paint, by adding a concentraed color to a can of white or colored paint, or by adding concentrated color or colors to a can of neutral "base" paint. And for those who don't want any guesswork there's the Color Carousel that mixes the paints right in the store. Whatever the method, the result is a range of colors such as no amateur painter has seen.

Mixing

Paste paints, such as aluminum, resin-emulsion, and lead-in-oil, should be stirred with a stiff paddle and reduced to painting consistency with the liquids recommended on the manufacturer's labels.

Paints in powdered form require the addition of a liquid to prepare them for use. The manufacturer's directions as to the amount of oil, varnish, water, or other vehicle required should be followed.

"Boxing" is a good method of mixing paints. Since paint is a mixture of solids and liquids, it is important that it be mixed thoroughly before using. To do this, the greater portion of the liquid contents of the can should be poured in a clean bucket somewhat larger than the paint can. Then, with a stiff paddle, the settled pigment in the original

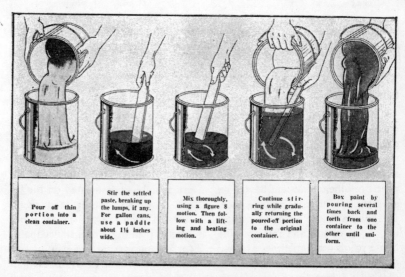

| Pour off thin portion into a clean container. | Stir the settled paste, breaking up the lumps, if any. For gallon cans, use a paddle about 1½ inches wide. | Mix thoroughly, using a figure 8 motion. Then follow with a lifting and beating motion. | Continue stirring while gradually returning the poured-off portion to the original container. | Box paint by pouring several times back and forth from one container to the other until uniform. |

Method of "boxing" or mixing paints.

Disposable dropcloths keep paint off shrubs and walks. Made of paper, they're cheap, light, won't damage bushes and flowers, can be used several times.

Rollers are quickly cleaned in tank of special fluid. Roller is simply dropped in and tank shaken like cocktail for one minute. New ring-shaped scraper is then slid along roller to squeeze out the excess cleaner.

Cleaning Up

Paper paint pails save buying and cleaning more expensive metal ones, are handy for mixing. Costing only a few cents, they're used once, then thrown away.

Waterless hand cleaner takes off both oil- and rubber-paint, will not irritate skin as solvents may. Paste is simply wiped on hands, then wiped off, taking paint with it.

container should be loosened and any lumps broken up. After this, mix the material in the container thoroughly, using a figure 8 motion, and follow with a lifting and beating motion. Continue stirring the mixture vigorously while slowly adding the liquid that was previously poured off the top. Complete the mixing by pouring the paint back and forth from one container to the other several times until the entire amount is of uniform consistency.

Paste and powder paints should be mixed in quantities sufficient for immediate use only, as these materials often become unfit for application if allowed to stand for three or more hours.

If paints have been allowed to stand and hard lumps or skin have formed, the skin or scum should be removed, after which the paint can be stirred and strained through screen wire or through one or two thicknesses of cheesecloth.

If a desired shade is not obtainable in custom- or ready-mixed paints, white paints may be tinted with colors-in-oil. To do this, mix the color-in-oil with a small amount of turpentine or mineral spirits and stir this into the white paint, a little at a time. If a blended color is desired, more than one color may be added, such as a chrome green and chrome yellow pigments to produce a lettuce green shade.

Painting—Basic Preparation of Surfaces

A satisfactory paint job requires cleaning, scraping, sanding, and puttying the surface prior to application of the paint. Do not try to cover chipped or cracked paint on woodwork. If dirt and rough spots are painted over, the new coating may peel, crack, blister, or wrinkle.

To prepare a surface for repainting, all loose paint should be removed with a putty knife or wire brush, rough spots sanded, and bare spots given a priming coat after the edges of the old paint film have been "feathered" or tapered off with sandpaper or steel wool. Nail holes should be filled with putty after the

priming coat is applied and, where a surface has been patched, the new surface should be primed before succeeding coats are put on.

To clean a painted surface that is cracked, checked, or "alligatored," paint remover should be applied with an all-hair brush and allowed to stand until the paint loses its adhesion. It can then be scraped off with a putty knife or paint scraper and wiped off with turpentine or mineral spirits. (See *Paint Remover.*) The spot can then be repainted.

New Interior Wood Surfaces

New interior wood surfaces generally can be cleaned simply by wiping with a rag soaked in solvent such as mineral spirits or turpentine. This will remove dust, greasy film and grimy dirt. If oil or wax has been spilled on the surface, re-

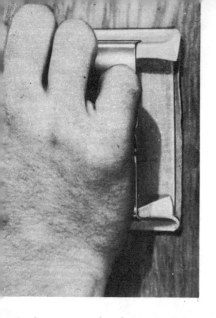

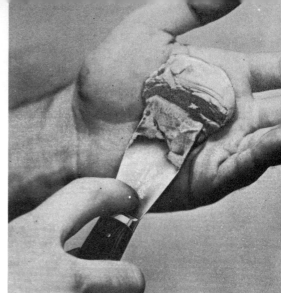

Sanding new wood surfaces smooth can be done effectively with a hand sanding block. Remember to sand with the grain finishing the job with #00 or finer paper. See **Abrasives**.

Any holes or cracks in the wood surfaces should be filled with wood putty, forced into the openings with a putty knife.

move by repeated solvent washings followed by immediate wipings with a clean, dry rag.

If the surface is to be varnished, shellacked, or finished in natural wood, sand to a smooth surface. Sand with the grain using #2 paper for rough and #00 or finer for finish sanding. Dust with a moist rag after sanding.

On open-grain woods such as oak, ash, hickory, mahogany and chestnut, apply one coat of clean or stained wood filler following manufacturer's directions. Close-grained woods such as maple, pine, cherry, or birch should be stained without filler. After the application of filler or stain and one coat of finish, putty-up nail holes and imperfections. Tint putty by mixing with small amount of stain and press into nail hole with thumb. Cut off with forward stroke of putty knife and smooth with a backstroke.

The reason that the filler or stain and one coat of finish are applied prior to puttying is to prevent the wood from absorbing the vehicle from the putty and becoming discolored. The absorption would also make the putty hard and brittle, eventually causing it to chip out.

If the surface is to be painted, sand as in the case of varnish, shellac or natural finish, wipe with moist cloth, apply one coat of wood primer, putty the imperfections, and follow with coat of enamel undercoat. Surface is then ready for any desired paint or enamel.

Painted Interior Wood Surfaces

Previously painted wood surfaces should be cleaned by wiping with a rag wet with a solvent such as mineral spirits or turpentine and immediately wiped dry with a clean rag. This should be done while the surface is wet, otherwise evapora-

tion of the solvent will simply redeposit the oils, grease, and dirt. If the surfaces are not waxed they may be cleaned with a solution of household kitchen detergent followed by thorough rinsing with clear water.

If the old paint or varnish is badly cracked, crazed, or wrinkled, it should be removed to the bare wood before repainting. This can be done with a chemical paint remover and 1½″ or 2½″ wood scraper. (See *Paint Remover.*)

Dirt should be cleaned from crevices and recesses using an "ogee" or "half ogee" scraper. If it is desired to remove moldings use a molding remover. It is good practice to scuff the surface of the old paint lightly with fine sandpaper, in the interests of better adhesion of the new paint.

On restaining work, particularly if the color of stain is to be changed, it is necessary to remove all old finishes down to the bare wood.

Where a stain color change is involved, try bleaching with a commercial wood bleach to lighten the stain that has penetrated into the wood. The surface should then be refinished as outlined above for new wood.

Plaster Walls

For new plaster walls, go over walls thoroughly to see that they are smooth, knocking off any mortar or plaster splotches with a 1¼″ putty knife. Remove all dust from walls with a vacuum cleaner. Allow

Sometimes it is necessary to remove old painted moldings. For example, if you wish to remove the paint and bleach the wood for a light natural finish. In such cases, use a molding chisel, shown here.

Old paint can be removed from wood by applying a chemical paint remover or heating the surface with a blowtorch and then scraping the painted film off with a putty knife.

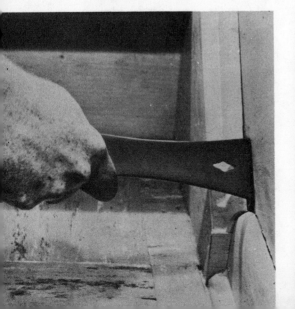

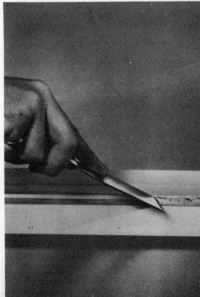

walls to season for 3 to 6 months before painting, or paint them with an alkali-resistant finish as the first coat.

Painted plaster walls should be cleaned, and cracks and broken areas repaired before repainting.

Peeling paint should be removed with a wall scraper.

To patch larger-than-hairline cracks (hairline cracks can be covered with sealer), first form a keyway for new plaster. Do not shape crack into a "V" because patched plaster later may fall out. Wide deep cracks should be filled with oakum or similar material to within ⅛" of the surface. Moisten crack before plastering. Spray water into the cracks, do not brush in. Brushing may sweep dirt into the base plaster and new plaster won't stick. Water can be sprayed into cracks by flicking from the end of a small brush. Apply plaster to cracks with a putty knife, the 1¼" size being recommended. Paint patched cracks color of walls or ceiling to prevent showing through when repainted.

To repair small cracks and broken areas, apply spackling (also spelled "spachtling"), which is somewhat like patching plaster, with a 5" spackling knife. For larger areas use patching plaster. Such patched areas should be sanded smooth the next day.

One coat of paint usually is sufficient although two sometimes are required. Two may be needed when going from a dark shade to a light shade or if the original paint is in very bad condition. Brush or roller may be used.

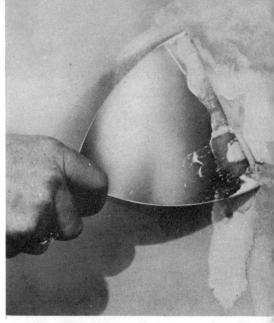

Photographs courtesy of Red Devil Tools.

Plaster walls should be prepared carefully and all holes and cracks filled. Spackling is best applied with a special 5" spackling knife, shown here, which resembles a putty knife but is much wider.

Preparation of Papered Walls for Painting

There are several ways to remove wallpaper, when required, before painting the wall (see later section on *Painting—Interior*).

Many people still use plain water, which will work after a fashion, but it is a slow and laborsome job. The warm water is applied with a sponge, brush or cloth. After the surface has been soaking for about 10 to 15 minutes, use a scraper to peel the paper off. Start at the top, keeping the blade against the wall. If the scraper is lifted at each stroke, it may nick the plaster or plasterboard each time it is reapplied and these nicks will have to be patched.

Removing old paint with a chemical paint remover is one way to insure a good painting job. This badly damaged exterior wood wall has had its paint removed with a chemical remover; once the paint film has softened, it's simple to remove it with a scraper or putty knife.

Removal of wallpaper is quick and easy with chemical wallpaper removers. Mix the concentrated solution with warm water and apply to the paper. Then scrape it loose without fear of damaging the surface of the wall proper.

Photographs courtesy of Wilson Imperial Co.

Many wallpapers made and sold in recent years have been "washable." This means that they resist water and permit washing. Therefore, plain water is not very effective when removing this type of wallpaper.

Wallpaper steamers (available on a rental basis from many hardware stores) have been in use for many years. They will do a good job of loosening the paper from the wall surface, but in the process they will saturate the entire room. Furthermore, if you have drywall construction, the steamer may loosen the protective top coat of the wall surfacing material itself.

Chemical wallpaper removers have gained in popularity because they are easier to use. Many of them are sold in concentrated form and are diluted in warm water. The solution can be applied with a brush, sponge or even a paint roller. After the paper has been saturated, it will peel off quickly and easily.

Outdoor Wood

The first step in preparing new outdoor wood surfaces for painting is to seal all knots with shellac or with the newer vinyl resin-type knot

sealers. Next, apply a prime coat of paint and then putty up all cracks and nail holes. Calk all joints and openings and proceed with final painting.

For painted outdoor wood surfaces, nail down all loose boards, preferably with aluminum nails, Countersink nails and fill nail holes with putty. Scrape off all loose or scaling paint. If old paint is peeling, checked or blistered, remove with tungsten carbide scraper; by burning with a torch and scraping with long handled putty knife or scraper; or by using a wax-free paint and varnish remover and scraper.

In repainting sash, scrape away loose putty, and prepaint the sash and that portion of the glass which will be covered by putty. Apply new putty when paint drys. Allow a few days for putty to harden.

Metal Surfaces

Remove peeling paint with carbide scraper and remove rust with emery cloth. Touch-up exposed areas with rust inhibitor, let dry and apply new paint. Allow new downspouts and gutters to stand a year before painting. They will oxidize and absorb paint better. If it is desired to paint immediately, age with strong vinegar or diluted acetic acid, wash clean and apply prime coat.

Masonry Walls

Peeling paint can be removed from smooth cement with a carbide scraper, or a wire brush may do the job on rough cement. If not, virtually nothing short of sand or steam blasting will do the job. Repaint when surface is clean and dry. (If there is a moisture or leakage problem, this must be corrected before painting.)

Painting—Brushes and Rollers

You have a choice of three different "tools" with which to paint.

• You can use the oldest and most common tool—the paint brush,

• or you can use the paint roller, which has advanced considerably in design since it was introduced about 1945,

• or there is the paint sprayer.

Which tool you use depends upon the job to be done and your skill. Here are some facts about each:

Brushes—Good quality brushes are not cheap, but a good brush, properly cared for, can last many years in the hands of a homeowner. Most handymen possess sufficient skill to use a brush but many do not know the fine techniques necessary for a professional-looking job. See section on *Brushes*.

Rollers—It is possible for the average homeowner to do a better paint job with a roller than with a brush. It is easy to develop the right skills and before you know it, you can work like a professional.

Sprayers—Considerable practice is needed in order to do a topnotch job with a sprayer. A poor sprayer in inexperienced hands will

BRUSH NOTES

Photographs courtesy of Pittsburgh Plate
Glass Co.

1. Select a quality brush for the job it is designed to do. Here (left to right) are: 1½" sash brush, 2" trim brush, 3½" and 4" wall brushes.

result in a poor job; so will a good sprayer in inexperienced hands. However, once you acquire the few simple skills, it is possible to do an outstanding job with a sprayer.

Covers for Rollers

The first practical paint-roller cover material, developed about 1945, was wool. However, after a great number of covers were used, it was found that wool did not provide a practical all-purpose cover. Sheep coming from different climates have different types of coats. The most desirable skin for a wool paint roller was a heavy, dense but medium-fine wool that was straight. Production methods were slow, because each skin had to be measured and only the select covers could be

cut out. The remainder was scrapped. All of this was done with hand labor.

Wool covers are fine for oil flat paints. They are useless in the new water and rubber base paints. Because wool absorbs roughly 14%, it soaks to the core, and the fibrous, resilient, paint-holding structure of the wool is lost, thereby making it worthless.

As a result, new fabric coverings were developed.

Dynel has the all-purpose characteristics needed to make a fine paint roller. It absorbs less than ½% water; therefore, it is excellent for water base paints. In oil base paints it works as well as wool. Because it is man-made, the denier and density of the cover are controlled to meet exact specifications.

2. When using a paint brush, dip it about half the length of the bristles into the can of paint. You should never get the ferrule (metal band) wet with paint.

3. Lightly wipe the excess paint off the brush by pressing it against the side of the can. Note that pressure is exerted just above the ends of the bristles.

4. Lay the paint on with short, slightly curved strokes, lifting the brush gradually at the end of the stroke. Note the correct way to hold the brush.

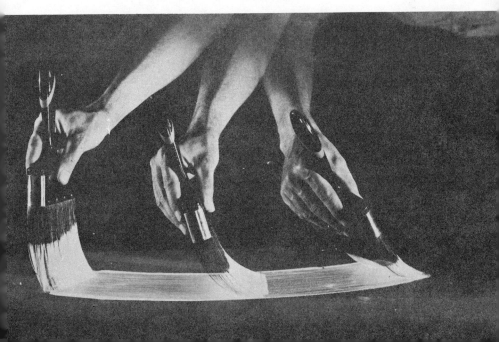

5. After you have finished painting, clean the brush thoroughly by submerging it and working the solvent well into the bristles. Use the right solvent for the paint.

6. Squeeze the bristles between the thumb and your fingers to work the paint out of the heel of the brush. It is essential not to leave any paint on the bristles.

7. After all the paint has been removed and the solvent squeezed out of the bristles, comb the brush. This will reset the bristles and keep them in working order.

8. When storing a brush, one that will be used again shortly, do not set it on its bristles! Instead, suspend it in a container or jar with solvent up to the ferrule.

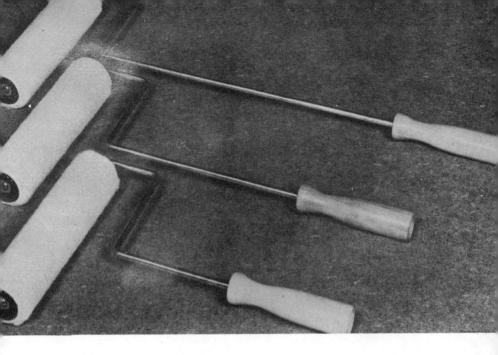

Dip-type rollers are made in a variety of sizes with different types of coverings designed for special surfaces. Here are three rollers, 14", 18" and 24" long; the length of the handle varies in order to enable you to reach out-of-the-way places.

Lonel is one of the finest of all synthetic paint roller fabrics on the market, and the most versatile. It is a fabric that will work in practically any kind of oil or water base paint, be it interior or exterior, gloss or flat.

The following paragraphs describe the specialized fabrics which have been developed to do specific jobs with special types of paint.

1. *Mohair*—Mohair rollers are short-nap rollers, less than ¼" in depth. This is a woven material that is specially designed to do a good job of applying heavy bodied enamels without showing a stipple.

2. *Dacron*—Dacron is the latest find in a roller material that is exceedingly fine in denier. It is woven into a cover that is especially designed to apply heavy-bodied exterior paints without showing an undue

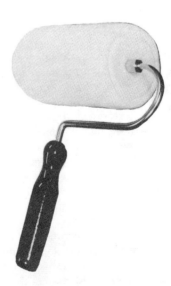

Fountain type rollers are often used by home handymen. Instead of dipping the roller into the tray to pick up the paint, the paint is poured into the cylinder.

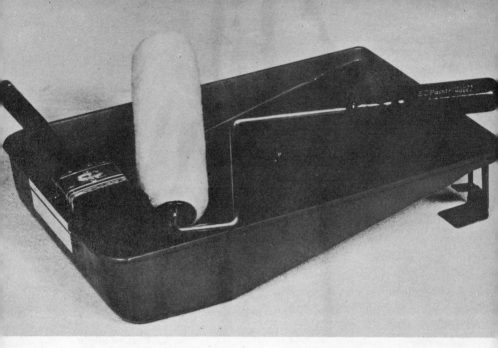

Dip-type rollers come with paint trays. This tray is used for interior painting and conveniently fits onto any step ladder. A special rest is available in order to hold a brush on the tray.

amount of stipple.

3. *Carpet and Fleecy Types*— These covers are used exclusively to apply oil-base paints. The different textures of these two fabrics produce different kinds of finishes, from sand float to Spanish textures.

4. *Sponge Rubber*—The sponge rubber roller accomplishes the same thing as carpet and fleecy types, but works successfully with water base texture paints.

The roller industry is constantly striving to develop and produce new types of fabrics that will apply paints better and faster than anything known before. Fabrics that are in test and have been used are: long cotton staples, Orlon, nylon, Acrilan, acrylics, etc.

Types of Rollers

Dip Roller—The most popular rollers developed are of the dip type. They range in size from 1″ to 13½″.

They work for such highly specialized uses as painting the underside of clapboard with the beveled 1″ roller (to be finished off with a 5½″ roller).

Corner rollers that are used to trace around ceilings, corners, and moldings prepare the way for 7″ or 9″ rollers which are used to finish the large surface of the wall.

There are 9″ to 13½″ rollers that are used for industrial purposes to cover large areas rapidly with the use of extension handles.

Floor to ceiling may be reached with 48″ handles, and greater distances may be reached with an aluminum, telescopic extension handle.

Short and long nap rollers made of the previously discussed fabrics are designed to paint almost any

For exterior use, a specially designed tray is used. It comes with a handy swivel hook which grips onto an outside ladder. Note the two different rollers; one is a "doughnut" shape used to paint inside of corners or edges of clapboard trim. The other is a 5½" dip-type roller for narrow surfaces, such as the face of clapboards.

type of surface, including smooth clapboard walls on the exterior of a house, shingles and stucco or masonry blocks.

Interior rollers can paint any type of wall construction. A roller applies the paint in an even paint film, applying only the proper amount of paint. Too little or too much paint cannot be applied with the roller, which works very much like a roller on a printing press. If a surplus of paint is applied to the wall, the roller will pick up the excess and apply it to a dry surface. When exactly the right amount of paint has been applied to a surface, the roller cannot pick this up and spread it out too thinly. In other words, a roller can apply just so much paint and no more. The amount put on is the correct amount.

Fountain Model Rollers—These are very practical to apply either flats or enamels to a wall. The advantage of a fountain model roller is that it eliminates dipping. Up to a pint of paint can be poured into a fountain roller, which is the reservoir for the excess paint. The cover is constructed to permit the paint to ooze through the fabric and be rolled onto the surface.

The first fountain rollers developed were constructed of metal, which made them heavy. Modern fountain rollers are constructed with nylon parts that are long-wearing, strong, and light. The inside fabric, which acts as the resilient part of the roller, is lonel, woven into a cushion,

and is covered with a sleeve of nylon which creates a thin, even, smooth surface with any kind of paint.

Pressure Rollers—These are designed wholly for professional use. Such rollers are ideally used in large buildings such as schools, hospitals warehouses, etc., where there are large surfaces, hallways, or rooms in which a single color is used. A pressure roller consists of a three-gallon material tank, from which an air-pressure pump ejects paint through a 15' hose and into the base of a 7" paint roller. The amount of paint that is allowed to flow into the roller is adjusted by a button in the handle. A pressure roller paints in a fraction of the time required by conventional methods, since it is basically designed for regulated, constant use.

Roller Cores

Construction of the various roller cover fabrics and their uses have already been discussed. However, there are three basic constructions of cores about which the covers are constructed:

1. *Wire* is superior to all other cores because of its plated, rust-proof characteristics. It can be re-used many times and formed into a perfect round shape when it is placed over the roller's adjustable drum. Wire is not affected by heat, cold, water, or oil.

2. *Plastic* cores constitute the middle quality of roller core construction. Plastic is practical. Because of its smooth inside diameter, it slips on and off roller handles quickly and easily. It is solvent-proof and durable.

3. *Fiber* cores are impregnated with waterproof and oilproof compounds to make them stand up in either water or oil base paints. They are lower in price than those of the two other cores. Because of its cheapness, fiber may be used once in a given color, then disposed of, rather than having to clean it for reuse. Fiber is serviceable and durable.

Roller Technique

As more and more Americans join the ranks of home decorators, the paint roller has become an important part of everyday life. Rollers now make it possible to paint expertly, with greater ease and with almost no mess. As with any job, a few rules of advance know-how can greatly lighten the task.

There is scarcely anything which the roller cannot paint easily and swiftly. Paint may be rolled right over wallpaper, plaster, wallboard, brick, clapboard, concrete, and other surfaces. Even wire fences can be painted by a long-nap roller.

Oil, rubber base, and water base paints can be used with equal success with rollers. These include flats, gloss and semi-gloss, enamels, sizing, varnish, aluminum paint, and shellac. Most of these can be used just as they come from the can. Ordinary instructions should be followed if thinning is needed.

The surface to be painted should be prepared as for any brush or spray painting: clean and free from oil, dust, or foreign matter. If the surface is new, a primer coat may be essential, but follow instructions on

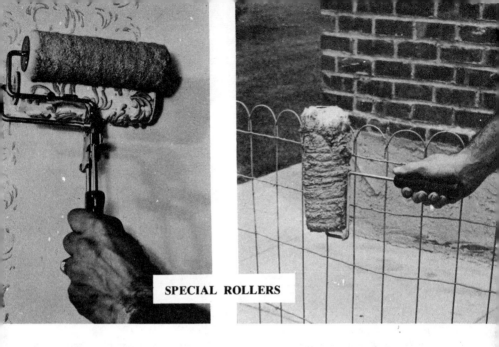

SPECIAL ROLLERS

You can paint your own patterns on the wall with a design roller. There are many different patterns available from which to choose. It works like an ordinary dip-type roller; the roller is soaked in paint and transfers the paint to the design roller, which in turn transfers the paint to the wall.

Wire fences are easy to paint in almost a single stroke. Extra long-nap rollers are used and, as they are rolled across the face of the wire fence, the paint is applied to the front and sides of the wires.

Photographs courtesy of E Z Paintr Corp.

the label of the finishing material to be used.

To begin painting, the roller tray, which can be placed conveniently on the floor or table, or attached to the ladder top or rung, should be filled to the "shore line," about half way up its slanted surface. Lining the tray with heavy paper or foil will save cleaning and permit quick changes of color.

Before actually painting the main surface area, a trim roller, a brush or one of several special devices which will be mentioned should be used progressively along the edges of the ceiling, floor, and woodwork. Do not trim the edges of more than one wall at a time, how-

ever. This will prevent shading.

The large roller should be loaded by rolling into the "shore line" of the paint, then back and forth on the ribbed surface of the tray to remove excess. Paint is applied to the surface with an easy back and forth rolling motion in any direction. Some "pros" recommend a criss-cross starting stroke. Be sure to keep the roller on the wall without spinning at the end of the stroke, and progress slowly and carefully into the previously trimmed edge, to within 1½″ of windows, corners, and edges.

"Roller" Aids

There are several devices which

If you have large surfaces to be painted, such as a patio floor or a basement floor, special rollers with handles are available for the job. The long nap of the rollers gets the paint into all the crevices.

More like a miniature blackboard eraser, this "roller" is designed for painting window sash trim. It's almost impossible to get paint on the glass.

provide the home decorator with invaluable supplementary tools to meet the problems of painting in corners and other hard-to-get-at areas. One of these is a 3"x5" wool surface padding which gives a finish of roller rather than brush consistency. A protective blade permits it to be used against ceiling, moldings, etc., without smearing. An extension handle facilitates painting behind radiators, pipes, and similar awkward spots.

Another device is a small felt surface mounted on a plastic handle. This can be drawn over window sash and other edges without allowing paint to run over. A guard blade prevents smearing. With such helpful gadgets as these, the need for masking tape is eliminated.

Painting ceilings, one of the messiest painting problems, is effortless with the long-handle roller. For greater than usual heights, there has recently been introduced a lightweight aluminum telescopic extension handle, to which a regular roller may be attached for reaching up to 14'.

There are three important tips for success in ceiling painting:

1. The roller should be worked easily back and forth across the narrowest dimension.

2. Care should be taken not to lift the roller from the surface nor to spin it.

3. Work should not be stopped until the entire ceiling is completed (this will prevent lapping).

There is no more bending, stoop-

ing, or tedious kneeling to floor painting with a long-handled roller or regular roller attached to an extension handle. Floors of concrete, wood, or linoleum can be covered with equal success.

Exterior Rollers

The exterior roller is versatile. Barns, silos, storage tanks, wagons, pens, picket fences, brick walls, boats, garden furniture, porches, and children's playthings are only some of the myriad things on which the exterior roller set can do a first-rate job.

Exterior paint rollers are similar to interior rollers, and may be cared for in the same way. Exterior rollers are generally larger, and the fabric is of a different type, to prevent the heavier bodied paints from stippling.

Here are a few precautions which, together with directions ordinarily found on paint cans, will produce really professional results in exterior painting.

New, unpainted wood surfaces should be allowed to dry thoroughly before painting. Knots and resin streaks should be sealed with a modern knot sealer or shellac to prevent bleeding or discoloration of paint film. Before painting old surfaces, loose paint should be removed with a scraper. Necessary repairs should be made: loose boards nailed down; projecting nail heads secured; cracks and nailhead pits filled in with putty. Finally, the area should be sanded smooth.

When preparing concrete surfaces it is important to remember that no paint will adhere to a loose, crumbly surface, so all loose part-

icles, dirt, etc., should be removed before painting. It is necessary to be sure that loose joints are routed out and "tuck pointed"; that cracks and crevices are filled; and that broken corners are replaced.

On clapboard walls the underedges should first be painted, one section at a time, with the small lap roller. Start at the top and work down. Follow with a 5½" roller on flat surfaces. Be sure that the roller contains no excess paint, and roll easily on the surface without spinning the end of the stroke.

If the surface of cement block or stucco is extremely rough, a long-nap roller is required. The long-nap roller is also effective on siding and shingles with deep crevices, as well as in such special work as painting wire fences.

Modern exterior roller trays have the gradually slanted surface of ordinary trays, but with a protective covering over the deeper end. Exterior trays may be attached to the sides of extension ladders, and fixed so that moving the ladder will not spill paint out of the tray. Still attached to the ladder, the tray may be moved to a vertical position and used as a pail for mixing paint. Another ladder lock permits the tray to be fastened to the top surface of a step ladder. This same ladder lock can be transposed into a carrying handle for the full tray when it is once again in vertical position.

Cleaning rollers has ceased to be a difficult problem. After the use of oil paint, the excess should first be squeezed out of the removable roller cover. This may be done without messiness by using a handy squeegee especially made for this purpose. Another tip: place the cover inside of a plastic or heavy paper bag and squeeze by hand.

Next, the roller cover should be saturated with a specially prepared roller cleaner, or turpentine, fuel oil, kerosene, or mineral spirits. The cover should be agitated in the solution, squeezed dry, then the process repeated. After painting with latex or water paint, the cover is similarly cleansed, but with soap in lukewarm water followed by a very thorough rinsing.

Before storing, remember to wipe the roller dry. Storing in a plastic container keeps covers fresh and clean for an indefinite period of time.

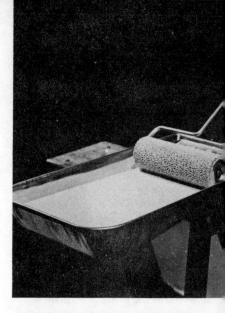

1. When using a roller, revolve it several times in the paint at the deep end of the tray. Then, get the surplus paint off the roller by squeezing it against the ramp of the tray.

HANDLING A ROLLER

2. Start the roller off with several criss-cross strokes on the area to be painted, then continue to work up and down to spread out the paint over the area.

Photographs courtesy of Pittsburgh Plate Glass.

3. After you have finished painting with a roller, clean it in the proper solvent. Agitate, squeeze out excess liquid and wipe the roller with a cloth. Then set cover aside to dry.

Painting—Common Failures and Their Cure

toring, Bleeding, Blistering, Chalking, Checking, Peeling, Spotting, Staining and *Wrinkling.*

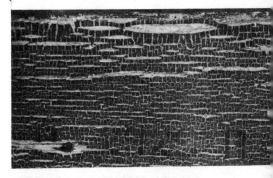

Alligatoring is an advanced form of checking, causing the paint film to take on the appearance of alligator skin, hence the name. It is usually caused by an improperly built-up paint film. Possibly, incompatible paints were used; perhaps the undercoat was not given sufficient time to dry; maybe the surface was never cleaned and the paint was applied over grease.

While it's true that no paint lasts forever, you have probably had some paints "fail" you. Within a matter of weeks or months, or even a year, there are imperfections, blisters; layers are peeling off. The term generally applied in such cases is "paint failure."

However, the chances are that it's not the paint's fault. Unless you have used an inferior paint, the cause of failure is either in your failure to prepare the surface properly to receive the paint or in your failure to apply the paint properly.

Of course, anyone who has wielded a paint brush immediately considers himself an experienced painter. Why, there's nothing to it— just put the paint on the brush and lay it on the surface. But painting is not that simple.

In the following parts of this section, there are detailed instructions on how to apply paint. For the present, however, let us concern ourselves with the "paint failures" and what we can do about them. Understanding why the paint failed is half the battle.

In the accompanying photographs, you will see some of the common types of paint failure. There is also information about possible causes together with information about cures. For more complete information, see sections on *Alliga-*

Blistering is a defect frequently caused by the construction of the house and not by the paint. It may be due to excessive moisture present behind the paint film. Maybe the wood was not dry when painted; maybe water seeped in behind the wood after it was painted and there is no way out but through the surface.

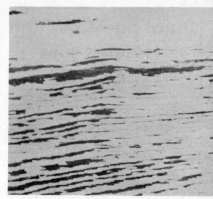

Checking is a minor paint failure; unless it is extensive, it can be ignored. It may be due to poor workmanship or the use of improperly formulated materials; maybe the undercoat was not dry when the final coat was applied. You can prevent checking by allowing sufficient drying time between coats. While some manufacturers say 24 hours are enough, it's better to wait 3 to 7 days between coats.

Cracking is sometimes caused by improperly made paints which dry too hard for the conditions of the particular job. The use of undercoats and finish coats of equal elasticity, possessing equal ability to expand and contract, will safeguard against this condition. Therefore, use the undercoat recommended by the manufacturer or one identical to it.

Staining is used to cover a variety of blemishes for which there are many causes. Water drips from metal (copper or iron pipe and gutters) can cause unsightly streaks. You can prevent this by painting the metal gutters and downspouts. Storm spots come from exposure to continuous rains and electrical storms. Usually weathering takes care of this damage and soon restores the original color to the paint film. When damp wood is painted, the water finds its way into the paint film carrying with it substances that cause brown stains. You can prevent this type of stain by making certain that the wood is seasoned and dry before painting. Structural defects must be watched for and eliminated; seal all knots to prevent the resin from seeping through and staining the paint film.

Spotting is caused by unequal oil absorption. A poor paint will soon show its weakness by extensive spotting. Adequate sealing of the surface is the secret of a good paint job. There is no economy in insisting on a low price paint or doing a shoddy job.

Wrinkling is a leather-like surface on a paint film. It can be caused by too heavy a coat of paint, improper brushing or it may be due to an improper combination of oil and pigment in the finish coat.

Photographs courtesy of Pittsburgh Plate Glass Co.

Paint Failure and Wood Rot

Sometimes paint failures are due to the improper preparation of the wood itself. Where wood is exposed to excessive moisture, more than paint is needed to keep it sound. It is best to treat the wood surfaces chemically to prevent wood rot and then paint over the treated wood.

See *Wood Rot.*

Painting—Exterior Surfaces

For exterior wood and metal surfaces, painting should be done only in clear dry weather and generally the temperature should not be below 50° F. When the weather is cold, work should be stopped early enough in the afternoon to allow the paint to set before a sudden drop in temperature occurs. Woodwork should be thoroughly dry and seasoned before paint is applied. Temperature conditions should be the same for painting exterior masonry as for wood and metal. Masonry surfaces must be dry if oil base paints are to be used, while other masonry paints such as cement-water and resin-emulsion may be applied to damp surfaces.

Sufficient time should be allowed between coats so that the paint film will dry hard before more paint is applied. Oil paints on exterior wood should dry at least 24 hours, several days' drying time being preferable.

USE THE RIGHT PAINT

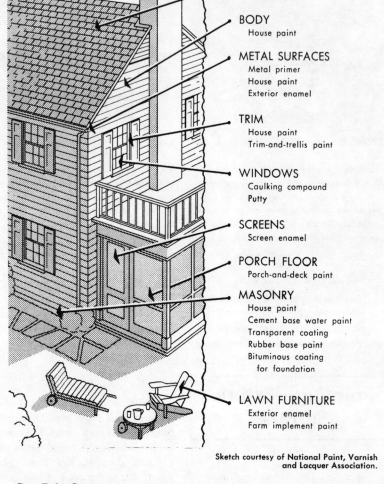

SHINGLES
Shingle stain

BODY
House paint

METAL SURFACES
Metal primer
House paint
Exterior enamel

TRIM
House paint
Trim-and-trellis paint

WINDOWS
Caulking compound
Putty

SCREENS
Screen enamel

PORCH FLOOR
Porch-and-deck paint

MASONRY
House paint
Cement base water paint
Transparent coating
Rubber base paint
Bituminous coating
  for foundation

LAWN FURNITURE
Exterior enamel
Farm implement paint

Sketch courtesy of National Paint, Varnish
and Lacquer Association.

Two-Coat Paint System

A minimum of three coats was formerly the accepted practice for initial painting on exterior wood, and this practice is still largely followed. However, by using special primers, two-coat paint systems for wood have been developed that are durable and satisfactory. The prin-ciple of the two-coat paint system is that as much paint is applied in two coats as normally would be applied in the three-coat method of painting. On smoothly planed wood, the usual spreading rate for three-coat painting is about 550 to 600 sq. ft. per gallon for the first or priming-coat

paint and about 600 to 650 sq. ft. per gallon for each of the next two coats. In the two-coat paint system, the primer is spread at the rate of about 450 sq. ft. per gallon and the finish coat about 550 sq. ft. per gallon. Rough surfaces and weather-beaten wood require much more paint than is indicated for smoothly planed wood.

Three-Coat Paint System

Mixed-pigment prepared paints are available for three-coat work, in addition to linseed-oil white-lead paints which may be mixed on the job or purchased ready-mixed. The manufacturer's directions should be followed in thinning the first and second coats. It is sometimes advisable in moist atmospheres, particularly at the seashore, to add a small amount (1 pint to a gallon) of good exterior varnish to the top coat of paint. The varnish should first be tried in a small amount of paint to make sure that the two are compatible and that the varnish will not cause the paint to thicken.

Shingle Stains

Shingle stains are pigmented oil stains, similar to very fluid paints, which can be applied by dipping, brushing, or spraying. They are intended for application to comparatively rough exterior wood surfaces where it is not necessary to bring out the grain and texture of the wood to which they are applied, and they dry to a matt or semi-transparent finish. Durable pigments, such as iron oxides, are used for the colors red through brown; chromium oxide, for green; and zinc oxide

Make certain that you cover all edges and spaces between boards when painting exterior wood.

Photograph courtesy of Valspar Corp.

or white lead tinted with lampblack, for gray.

Shingle stains should not cake or change color in the container and when stirred should settle very slowly. With the exception of some dark brown stains, which are simply refined coal-tar creosote with volatile thinners, shingle stains are usually made from very finely ground pigments, drying oils, and volatile thinners. Many commercial shingle stains contain some creosote oil from coal tar or water-gas tar which is intended to act as a wood preservative. While pressure treatment with creosote is one of the most effective methods of preventing wood from rotting, the small amount that penetrates the wood from a single dip or brush treatment probably has very little effect.

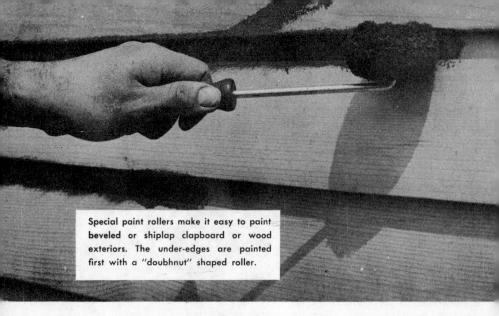

Paint applied over creosote stain is likely to be ruined by the creosote bleeding through. If there is any possibility that the shingles may be painted at some future time, pigment oil shingle stains without creosote should be used.

Masonry Surfaces

Paints for masonry wall surfaces may be divided into four types: Cement water paint, resin-emulsion paint, oil paint, and paint containing rubber in the vehicle. These paints are also suitable for use on such masonry surfaces as foundations, gate posts, and fence or enclosure walls, but they should not be used on floors which are subject to abrasion. For such surfaces, a very hard-drying paint with good water resistance and gloss retention is recommended.

Cement-water paints are water-dilutable paints in which Portland cement is the binder. They are particularly suitable for application on

Photographs courtesy of E Z Paintr Corp.

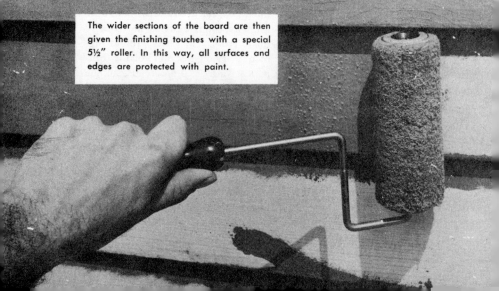

damp, new, or open-textured masonry surfaces. These surfaces include those walls that are damp at the time of painting, or that may become damp after painting as a result of structural defects or other causes; new structures (less than 6 months old) which normally contain water-soluble alkaline salts; and open-textured surfaces such as cinder, concrete, and lightweight aggregate block. These paints are not recommended for stopping leakage through porous walls that are exposed to water pressure, particularly if the paint is applied to the inside of the wall. For such conditions, a coating of hot bituminous material applied to the outside of the wall is preferable.

Close-textured surfaces which are relatively dry, such as cast concrete, asbestos-cement siding, and tile, may be painted with resin-emulsion paint or paints containing rubber in the vehicle. Walls which are dry at the time of painting, and are so constructed as to remain dry after painting, may be decorated satisfactorily with oil paints.

CEMENT-WATER PAINT

Cement-water paints are water-dilutable paints, packaged in powder form. They are composed chiefly of Portland cement or Portland cement and lime and possess good decorating qualities or hiding power and color. However, when wetted, as by rain, they become somewhat translucent and darker in color. When again dry, the film returns to its original opaqueness and color.

To clean a surface for the application of cement-water paint, thoroughly remove all dust, dirt, and efflorescence, old coatings of whitewash, and flaking or scaling cement-water paint by brushing vigorously with a wire brush. Firmly adhering coatings of cement-water paint or cement-water paints which are "chalking" or "dusting" need not be removed, but should be brushed with a stiff bristle brush to make the surface uniform.

Before applying the paint, whether initially or on a previously painted surface, the masonry should be thoroughly wetted, preferably with a garden hose adjusted to produce a fine spray. A superficial dampening with a brush dipped in water is not adequate for exterior walls but may be satisfactory for cool basement walls. Usually, wetting the walls in one operation not more than an hour before painting is sufficient. The water should be applied so that each part is sprayed three or four times for about 10 seconds each, time being allowed between applications for the water to soak into the surface. If the surface dries rapidly, as it may in hot weather, it should be redampened slightly just before painting. The wall surface should be moist, not dripping wet when paint is applied.

Cement-water paint powder should be mixed with water in accordance with the manufacturer's directions. Paints may be tinted by adding suitable amounts of coloring pigments but, due to the difficulty of producing uniform colors by hand mixing, it is suggested that commercial brands of tinted paints be purchased which have been mill ground in the factory.

Paint rollers can be used to cover brick. It is best to use a long nap roller so that the paint covers the brick surfaces and the mortar joints as well.

Cement-water paint should be applied in two coats. Preferably not less than 24 hours' drying time should be allowed between coats. The first coat should be slightly moistened with water before applying the second.

Most Portland cement paints cannot be satisfactorily applied with the ordinary hair-bristle paint brush. Proper application requires a brush with relatively short, stiff, fiber bristles such as fender brushes, ordinary scrub brushes, or roofers' brushes.

While thick films are to be avoided, there is a tendency to use too much water in cement-water paint and to brush it out too thin. Coatings applied in this manner may look well at first but will generally lose their opacity and protective value much sooner than thicker films. The proper spreading rate is difficult to estimate for Portland cement paint because of the difference in the texture of the masonry to be covered. However, on smooth masonry, 1 gallon of mixed paint should be sufficient to cover 100 sq. ft. with two coats; and, for rough masonry, 1 gallon should be sufficient to apply two coats to 50 sq. ft. of surface.

After painting, it is desirable to sprinkle the freshly painted surface two or three times a day with a fog spray, such as is used for dampening walls prior to painting, and it is recommended that this be done between coats and for 2 days after the final coat, starting as soon as the paint has set, usually 6 to 12 hours after application.

RESIN-EMULSION PAINT

Resin-emulsion paints are water-thinned materials whose dry-film properties closely resemble those of a flat oil paint. They may be used on most porous masonry surfaces, including asbestos-cement siding, which has not been previously coated with a waterproofing compound. They should not be used on magnesite stucco.

To prepare the surface for resin-emulsion paints, remove by brushing or washing all dust, dirt, efflorescence, and loose particles from the surface; and also remove any flaking or scaling paint by scraping or wire brushing. Glossy areas should be dulled by sanding; oil, grease, and

wax should be removed by scrubbing with mineral spirits. Then wash with water containing trisodium phosphate (about 2 ounces to the gallon), and rinse thoroughly with clean water.

Resin-emulsion paints are packaged in paste form and need to be thinned with water before being applied. They should be mixed in clean metal containers (not wood) in accordance with the directions given on the manufacturer's label and not allowed to stand after mixing for more than a week.

Resin-emulsion paint should be applied in two coats and the air temperature when painting should be above 50° F. A sizing or priming coat is not generally required except on open-textured masonry. For that, a cement-water paint containing sand should be used to fill the voids in the wall surface. On very warm days, it may be advisable to moisten the surface to be painted with water, prior to applying the paint. Resin-emulsion paint will dry in 1 to 4 hours, and may be recoated in 6 to 8 hours; the film becomes hard overnight. One gallon of the paste paint will cover approximately 200 to 450 sq. ft., depending upon the surface and the application. Brushes and spray guns should be washed with warm soapy water immediately after using.

OIL PAINTS

Oil paints intended for use on masonry are usually ready-mixed paints containing weather-resistant opaque pigments suspended in drying oils, resins, and thinners. They should be formulated so that the first coat seals the surface sufficiently to prevent spots or flashes of the second coat. Two coats are necessary for good hiding and durability.

Moisture back of the paint film will seriously impair the life of a coating of oil-base paint, therefore the application of oil paint to new masonry should be deferred until the walls have had time to dry. This may require 3 months to a year, depending upon the thickness and porosity of the wall and the weather conditions. Because of the importance of preventing water from entering the walls after painting, repairs of structural defects, such as leaks around flashing, doors, and windows, should be made before applying oil-base paint.

Dust and dirt should be washed off and efflorescence should be brushed off with a stiff fiber or wire brush. All traces of oil should be removed with steel brushes, abrasive stones, or a lye solution. However, if the surface is badly stained, it should be lightly sandblasted.

Caution:—When using lye (caustic soda, sodium hydroxide), avoid splashing the eyes, skin, and clothing because it may cause burns.

Old coatings of organic paint or cement-base water paint in sound condition need not be removed. Whitewash or peeling, scaling, or flaking paints should be completely removed.

Oil paints should not be applied during damp or humid weather or when the temperature is below 50° F. At least 1 week of clear dry weather should precede the application of the first coat. As masonry surfaces tend to chill and collect

It's easy to paint rough concrete with a roller. This is a job that would take a long time and ruin a paint brush. But with a roller, you can apply the paint just as easily as if you were painting a flat interior wall.

Photograph courtesy of E Z Paintr Corp.

condensed moisture, painting early in the morning and late afternoon should be avoided except in dry climates.

A minimum of 90 days' drying time should elapse before applying oil paint over a cement-water base or over mortar-filled joints and cracks. When it is not practicable to wait this long before painting, a calking compound rather than cement mortar should be used as a crack filler.

RUBBER-BASE PAINTS

There are two types of rubber-base paints, the rubber-solution and rubber-emulsion types.

Rubber-solution paints are available at most paint stores and usually sell for slightly more than oil-base masonry paints. They may be applied by brush, spray or roller to dry or slightly damp walls. They are suitable for painting asbestos-cement siding and shingles. These paints are also useful for "sealing in" stains on old masonry, and as protective primers under finishing coats of resin-emulsion or oil-base paints.

The same procedure outlined for preparing the surface for oil-base paints should be followed for rubber-base paints in removing dust, dirt, loose mortar, form oil, and efflorescence on dense surfaces.

Oil paint coatings must be removed before applying rubber-solution paints because the thinners used in these paints act as solvents for the oil paints. This is not necessary when applying rubber-emulsion paints over oil paints that are in good condition since they do not contain solvents that will soften oil paints.

Rubber-base paints may be applied to dry or damp walls. It is usually necessary to thin the paint for the first coat, using the thinner recommended by the manufacturer, as some paint thinners are incompatible with rubber-base paints. The paint dries to the touch within three hours but, at least 18 hours' drying time should be allowed between coats, otherwise the succeeding coat will "lift" or soften the undercoat.

The brushing technique for rubber-base paints is the same as for applying enamels. "Back-brushing" or "working" the paint will cause it to roll and pull under the brush. As the

paint tends to "set" rather quickly, it is advisable to work in shade rather than sunlight.

Brushes and spray guns should be cleaned with paint thinner immediately after they are used, because dry paint is difficult to redissolve once it has hardened.

Iron and Steel Surfaces

The chief reason for applying paint to exterior metalwork, particularly iron and steel, is to control and prevent corrosion. For best results two coats of priming paint followed by two coats of top or finishing paint are recommended on new work. For repainting, a spot coat followed by a full priming coat, and then one or two finish coats are recommended. The usual recommended spreading rate of each coat of paint is about 600 sq. ft. per gallon. It should be stressed that the preparation of the surface, particularly steel, prior to painting is important, for unless the surface is properly cleaned so that the priming paint comes in direct contact with the metal, early failure of the paint film will probably occur.

Cleaning is the most important step in preparing metalwork for painting. It can be divided into two phases; the removal of oil and grease, and the removal of rust, dirt, scale, old paint, and moisture. All oil and grease should be removed before using mechanical methods of cleaning. The usual method is to wipe the surface with clean cloths and mineral spirits or carbon tetrachloride. The liquid as well as the cloths should be kept clean by frequent renewals to avoid leaving a thin, greasy film on the surface. When the oil and grease have been disposed of rust, scale, and old paint may be cleaned from the surface with wire brushes, steel wool, or motor-driven rotary brushes.

The paint should be applied in bright, warm weather to metal surfaces which are clean and dry. Painting should not be done early in the morning when the surface to be painted is damp from dew. Ample time should be allowed for each coat of paint to dry before applying the next coat.

Since the main function of a priming coat is to protect metal from corrosion, it should contain rust-inhibitive pigments. It can be applied by either brush or spray but particular care should be taken to cover the surface completely with the proper thickness of paint. Two coats of primer are recommended for new work. The second coat may be tinted to a slightly different color to make sure of adequate surface coverage. Ample time should be allowed for drying before application of succeeding coats.

Two practical coatings for steel surfaces are red-lead and iron oxide paints, red lead being used as a primer and iron oxide as a finishing material. Dull red and brown iron-oxide paints are economical for painting terne-plate roofs and structural metal. They are durable and are frequently referred to as roof and barn paint.

Red lead is available in three types: Type I, red-lead linseed oil paint which should be allowed to dry for a week between coats; type II, semi-quick-drying red-lead paint

Photographs courtesy of E Z Paintr Corp.

which is an easy brushing material suitable for general use and dries in 24 hours; and type III, red-lead paint in a varnish vehicle which dries within 8 hours and may be used for touch-up work on clean smooth steel.

Zinc-dust primers have good rust-inhibitive properties and are particularly effective for galvanized iron and sheet zinc. While the primary function of these paints is to provide adequate adherence on galvanized metal, they are also satisfactory as finish paints and may be used in one or more coats.

Quick-drying metal primers for home workshop machinery and automobiles are iron-oxide primers in which the vehicle is a thin varnish. They dry to a smooth velvety, flat eggshell finish, and give excellent foundations for decorative coats.

As finish coats on iron or steel, black and dark-colored paints are more durable than light-tinted paints. Red-lead paint should not be used as a final coat, since it does not retain its color. One of the best finish coats for metal is aluminum

It just isn't possible, nor is it safe, to try to hold a paint tray in one hand and paint with the other when standing on a ladder. However, special trays are made for outdoor use; they attach conveniently and easily on the ladder.

paint made by mixing about 2 lbs. of aluminum powder or paste with 1 gallon of spar varnish.

Copper

Copper gutters and flashings, as well as copper or bronze screening, may cause yellowish-green stains on light- or white-painted houses. One way to avoid this is to paint or varnish the copper or bronze. The surface of the metal should be cleaned by washing with gasoline or turpentine, and a priming coat composed of 1½ to 2 lbs. of aluminum powder to 1 gallon of aluminum mixing varnish applied, followed by the desired color coat. Weathered copper or bronze fly-screening should be dusted and then given two coats of thin black enamel. Zinc dust-zinc oxide paints may also be used on copper and bronze if a gray color is acceptable.

Planning to paint the outside of your house?
Here are some color suggestions for you.

If your house has shutters, paint the trim the same color as body of house—or white. If not, use these suggested colors for trim.

If the roof of your house is	You can paint the body	...and the trim or shutters and doors														
		Pink	Bright red	Red-orange	Tile red	Cream	Bright yellow	Light green	Dark green	Gray-green	Blue-green	Light blue	Dark blue	Blue-gray	Violet	Brown	White
GRAY	White	X	X	X	X	X	X	X	X	X	X	X	X	X	X		
	Gray	X	X	X	X		X	X	X	X	X	X	X	X	X		X
	Cream-yellow		X		X		X			X	X						X
	Pale green				X		X			X	X						X
	Dark green	X				X	X	X									X
	Putty			X	X			X	X			X	X			X	
	Dull red	X				X		X					X				X
GREEN	White	X	X	X	X	X	X	X	X	X	X	X	X	X	X		
	Gray			X		X	X	X									X
	Cream-yellow		X		X			X	X	X						X	X
	Pale green			X	X		X		X								X
	Dark green	X		X		X	X	X									X
	Beige			X					X	X	X		X	X			
	Brown	X				X	X	X									X
	Dull red					X		X		X							X
RED	White		X		X			X			X			X			
	Light gray		X		X			X									X
	Cream-yellow		X		X						X	X	X				
	Pale green		X		X												X
	Dull red					X		X		X	X						X
BROWN	White			X	X		X	X	X	X		X	X	X	X		
	Buff				X				X	X	X				X		
	Pink-beige				X				X	X					X	X	
	Cream-yellow					X			X	X	X				X		
	Pale green								X	X					X		
	Brown		X			X	X										X
BLUE	White		X	X		X						X	X				
	Gray		X		X							X	X				X
	Cream-yellow		X	X									X	X			
	Blue		X			X	X					X					X

To paint clapboards, first run your brush along the edge where one strip of siding overlaps the next. Then "spot-paint" a strip of the siding by striking your newly-filled brush to the wood at intervals. Join the spots with smooth brush action that spreads the paint evenly, making sure that you cover the entire board.

Paint the trim before painting the siding on upper sections of a house where you need to use a ladder. This eliminates the danger of marring newly painted surfaces with the top of the ladder. On lower sections of a house, the siding can be painted before the trim.

At right, the man of the household works on the trim, while the shutter receives feminine attention.

Before the finish coat is applied, all surfaces must be carefully prepared. Rough spots should be sanded smooth; all rust removed. Cracks should be filled. Any spots of bare wood or metal must be primed.

How to Paint a Clapboard House

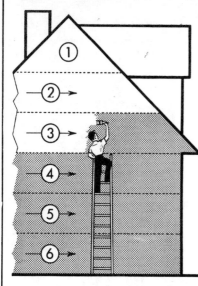

When painting the side of a house, start at the highest point and apply paint in horizontal strips about 3 feet wide, working from left to right. When possible, paint above the top of the ladder. This enables you to reach a wider area. Never stop in the middle of a strip for any great length of time. For safety and working ease, the distance between the house and the base of your ladder should be about 1/4 to 1/3 of the ladder's length.

1. Load your brush, then apply two or three dabs of paint along the joint of the siding. This helps to distribute the paint quickly and easily.

2. Next, brush the paint out well, being sure to coat the clapboard under-edge.

3. "Feather" the ends of your brush strokes so the coat will be smooth where one section joins another.

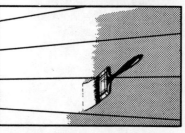

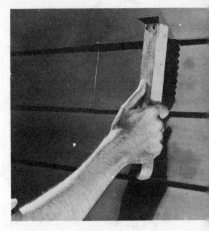

Check exterior wood siding and wood trim for loose paint. You can remove small areas with sandpaper and sanding block.

A wire brush comes in handy to remove any grime and surface dirt before applying the paint.

10 Steps to Successful Outdoor Painting

Where necessary, calk joints around windows, doors and chimneys. You can do this with a putty knife and calking compound or it's easier and quicker to do a better job with a calking gun. See **Calking**.

Check around the window panes for loose putty. If any is missing or loose, replace it with sound putty. See **Glazing**.

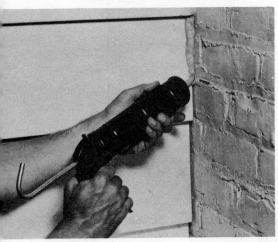

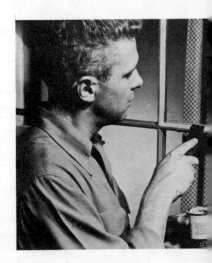

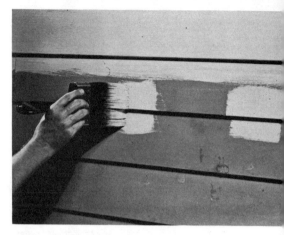

Start painting on the outside at the highest part of the house. Make certain that the ladder is secure before you climb it. See **Ladders**.

Lay brushload of paint on in two or three places and then brush out well. Note that you never soak the entire brush in paint; do not get ferrule wet.

Photographs courtesy of Pittsburgh Plate Glass Co.

When painting clapboard or beveled or shiplap siding, always paint the edges first, using the brush on its flat side, never its edge. You can do the same job with special rollers.

After brushing out the paint, finish with tips of the brush to a thin feather-edge. Now continue to lay on brushloads of paint, working from the wet edge outward.

Photographs courtesy of Pittsburgh Plate Glass Co.

When painting around window sash outside the house, keep the sash brush well loaded for full-bodied stroke. In this way, you will be able to do a better job with less smearing of paint on the glass.

If the surface coat of gutters and downspouts is still good, you can apply the final coat immediately. Otherwise, it is essential that a prime coat be applied before the final coat.

Painting—Interior

Interion painting requires as careful preparation of surfaces as does exterior painting. The advent of odorless paints now makes it possible to paint any time of the year. Formerly, most interior painting in the home was done in the fall or spring, when it was possible to leave the windows open to ventilate the room. But open windows brought dust into the room to mar the finished painted surface.

A good interior paint job is often 50% preparation and 50% painting. Do not rush in preparing the surfaces in your eagerness to get at the brush or roller. If you do not prepare the surfaces properly, you'll be back with the paint brush or roller in a few months.

It is recommended that you re-read the section on *Painting—Basic Preparation of the Surfaces*. Then, in this section you will find the necessary information on the application of different types of paints on various interior wall, ceiling and floor materials.

Plaster

New dry plaster in good condition, which is to be finished with a paint other than water paint, should be given a coat of primer-sealer and

allowed to dry thoroughly before being inspected for uniformity of appearance. Variations in gloss and color differences in the case of tinted primers indicate whether or not the whole surface has been completely sealed. If not, a second coat of primer-sealer should be applied. If only a few "suction spots" are apparent, a second coat over these areas may be sufficient.

A flat, semigloss, or high-gloss finish may be applied to the primed surface. For a flat finish, two coats of flat wall paint should follow the priming coat. For a semi-gloss finish, one coat of flat wall paint and one coat of semi-gloss paint should be applied to the primed surface. For a high-gloss finish, one coat of semi-gloss paint and one coat of high-gloss enamel should be used over the priming coat.

Before applying water paints of the calcimine type to new plastered walls they should be sized, using either a glue-water size or, if the plaster is dry, a thin varnish or primer-sealer. Cold water paints of the casein type may be applied either directly to a plastered surface, or the surface may be first given a coat of primer-sealer to equalize uneven suction effects. The same is true of resin-emulsion paints, with the recommendations of the manufacturer of the product being given preference in case of doubt. Since resin-emulsion paints usually contain some oil in the binder, they should ordinarily be applied only to plaster which has dried thoroughly.

Texture wall paints may also be used on plaster surfaces. The ad-

PAINTING POINTERS

Avoid a ring of paint where you put down can by keeping a paper plate under it. Daub a little paint on the bottom of can, press the plate against it and the plate will stick.

Unpainted furniture should first be sealed by brushing a very thin wash coat of shellac on the raw wood. When dry, smooth lightly with sandpaper. Apply undercoat, brush out thoroughly, let dry at least 24 hours and sand again. Apply finish coat with smooth, light brush strokes, using just the tip of the bristles.

Fit a disk of window screening inside can after mixing paint well. As the screen sinks, it will carry lumpy paint particles to bottom.

These paintbrush defects all result from misuse of the brush: Painting with side of brush is a major cause of "fingering." If you use a wide brush to paint pipes and similar surfaces it will take a fishtail shape. Swelling may occur if you dip the brush too deeply. If paint hardens in the heel, it will swell the ferrule. Avoid curling by hanging the brush up.

PAINTING POINTERS

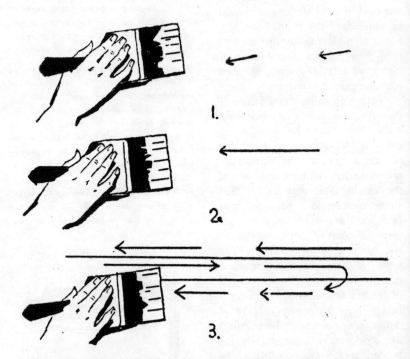

In painting exterior surfaces, you can get a smoother and more uniform job by daubing paint on in spots (1) before stroking. Then use long, leveling brush strokes (2) to spread the paint smoothly. Finish the brush stroke (3) in a zigzag path and you'll have a good-looking job.

Keep bugs out of wet paint applied outdoors by adding insect repellent to each batch that you mix.

Save priming time by using the widest brush you can for each job. A 4" brush is the most popular width for large, flat surfaces. Use a trim or sash brush, available in 1" to 3" widths, for woodwork, paneling and trim. For narrow table legs and chair rungs, use the narrowest sash brush. A sash brush may be flat or oval.

Remove knobs or handles and other hardware. You'll find it easier to brush paint smoothly on drawer fronts and cabinet doors. Attach knobs to cardboard as shown above and paint them with a small brush.

Keep bristles pointed downward, or at least tilted at an angle below the horizontal, while you work. Tilt a brush upward only for ceiling work. Pointing the bristles down helps keep paint from running into the heel. If the paint hardens in the heel it will swell the ferrule and perhaps ruin the brush. For the same reason, dip a brush no more than halfway into paint each time you charge it.

Blend each stroke toward the wet paint area, not away from it, to avoid ridges and lap marks.

PAINTING POINTERS

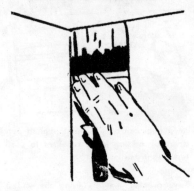

Angle your brush into corners; never paint with its sides. Angling in protects the bristles and gives you a smoother, more even finish.

• • •

You can lengthen the life of a fine, pure bristle brush by using it only to apply finish coats. Keep brushes with synthetic or mixed bristles handy for priming and for use on rough surfaces that wear down bristles fast.

• • •

Use masking tape where two shades are to meet. Paint on one color, let it dry, apply tape at the dividing line and then brush on the second color. The result will be a neater job and you'll save time.

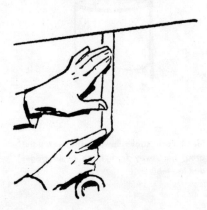

vantages of this type of paint are that one coat economically produces a textured decoration and relieves the monotony of smooth flat paint. It also covers cracks or patches in the plaster more completely than ordinary wall paint. The disadvantages of texture wall paint are that they collect dust and are difficult to restore to a smooth finish. These materials are available as water- or oil-base paints, are thicker than ordinary wall paints, and may be applied to wallboard as well as plaster to produce textured effects such as random, Spanish, mission, and multicolored.

For more information, see the section on *Plaster*.

Composition Wallboard

Composition wallboard usually presents no particular painting difficulties if the ordinary precautions are observed, such as making certain that the surface is dry and free from grease and oil. The painting procedure for wallboard is the same as for plaster; it requires a priming and sealing coat followed by whatever finish coats are desired, or may be given one-coat flat or resin-emulsion type paint.

Wallpaper

Water-thinned paint may be applied to wallpaper that is well-bonded to the wall and does not contain dyes which may bleed into the paint. One thickness of wallpaper is preferable for paint application. Paints other than those of the water-thinned type may also be applied to wallpaper by following the directions given for painting

plaster. However, wallpaper coated with such a paint is difficult to remove without injury to the plaster.

Wood Walls and Trim

New interior walls and wood trim should be smoothed with sandpaper and dusted before painting or varnishing. To preserve the grain of the wood, the surface may be rubbed with linseed oil, varnished or shellacked, and waxed. If an opaque finish is desired, semi-gloss paint thinned with 1 pint of turpentine per gallon of paint or the primer-sealer previously described for walls may be used as a priming coat on wood. One or two coats of semi-gloss paint should then be applied over the thoroughly dry prime coat, or if a full-gloss finish is desired, the last coat should be a high-gloss enamel.

Wood Floor Finishes

For information on varnishing wood floors, refer to the section on *Floors, Wood—Finishing.*

Masonry Walls and Ceilings

Interior masonry walls and ceilings above grade may, in general, be painted in much the same manner as plaster surfaces. Here again,

PAINTING POINTERS

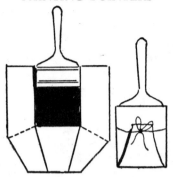

Wrap brush for storage, using heavy paper, oilcloth or aluminum foil. Be sure that the bristles lie straight and that end of brush is not compressed by the wrapping. Suspend the brush with the bristles down. If it's a fine-quality brush used in oil paints, saturate the brush with linseed oil before wrapping it.

Brush storage rack can be made by driving short nails part way into ¾" plywood so brushes can rest on handles. Mount board on door or shop wall. Wrap brushes before storage.

Store brushes in solvent overnight, suspending them in the container by one of the methods illustrated here. In method at far right, the handle is tied to thin stick extending beyond bristles. Brush can then stand upright without resting on bristles.

Sketches courtesy of Baker Brush Co.

Easy way to avoid cleaning the tray afterwards is to line it with aluminum foil before you pour the paint into it. Use a fairly thick piece of foil or several sheets of the household type.

it is necessary to allow adequate time for the masonry to dry before applying paint and, in addition, attention should be given to the preparation of the surface. When decorating a wall containing Portland cement (concrete, for example), it is essential to take precautions against the attack of alkali. For this purpose, alkali-resistant primers such as rubber-base paints may be used when oil paints are to follow.

Cement-water paints are best suited for application to basement walls which are damp as a result of leakage or condensation. To apply these paints, the same procedure should be followed as is described here for painting exterior masonry walls.

Concrete Floors

Two general types of paints for concrete floors are varnish and rubber-base paint. Each has its limitations and the finish cannot be patched without the patched area showing through. Floor and deck enamel of the varnish type gives good service on concrete floors above grade where there is no moisture present.

Rubber-base paints, which dry to a hard semi-gloss finish, may be used on concrete floors below grade, providing the floor is not continually damp from seepage and condensation.

With a roller, you can cover a large area at one time and make certain that you are applying the right amount of paint—not too much and not too little.

Paint should not be applied to a concrete basement floor until the concrete has aged for at least a year. The floor should be dry when painted, the best time for application being during the winter or early spring (assuming there is some heating apparatus in the basement), when the humidity in the basement is low. In general, three coats of paint are required on an unpainted floor, and the first coat should be thin to secure good penetration. After the paint is dry, it should be protected with a coat of floor wax.

In repainting concrete floors, where the existing paint has been waxed and is in good condition except for some worn areas, the surface should be scrubbed with cloths saturated with turpentine or petroleum spirits and rubbed with steel

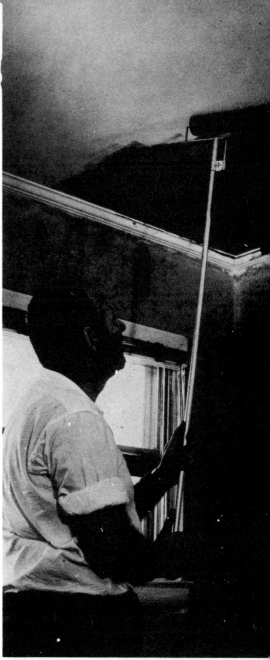

Special rollers make two-color painting easy. This is a blackboard type of roller with a plastic shield along one edge. In this way, it is easy to apply one color paint to the wall and another to the trim and still get perfectly straight line between them without intermixing the colors.

No more standing on a plank in the air or climbing up and down a ladder to paint a ceiling. A convenient extension handle is attached to the ordinary roller. It makes it easy to reach the ceiling while standing on the floor.

Photographs courtesy of E Z Paintr Corp.

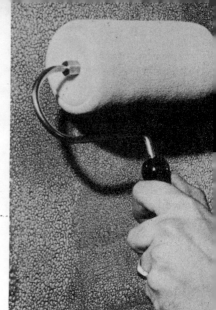

Getting into corners is always a problem! Working a brush into a corner may result in splashed and spattered paint. An ordinary roller just won't get all the way in. The "doughnut" is just the right answer.

For a stippled effect, you can use a roller with a special cover that will produce the stipple effect with enamel paint. Here, a stipple coat is being applied over glass.

Two-tone painting is simple with a roller on textured plywood. The base or first coat is applied with a long nap roller, making certain that you work the paint into all the crevices.

The top or second coat is applied with a short-nap roller that just skims over the surfaces. The paint stays on the raised portions of the textured plywood while the base or bottom coat remains untouched.

wool while wet, to remove all wax before repainting. If this is not done, the paint will not adhere and dry satisfactorily. If the old paint is badly worn, it should be removed by treating with a solution of 2 lbs. of caustic soda (household lye) to 1 gallon of hot water. This may be mopped on the surface and allowed to remain for 30 minutes after which the floor can be washed with hot water and scraped with a wide steel scraper. Another method of application is to spread a thin layer of sawdust, which has been soaked in caustic solution over the floor and allow it to stand overnight. The following morning, the floor can be washed with hot water and the paint scraped off. The surface should then be rinsed thoroughly with clean water.

If you're looking for a place to rest that brush, here's a handy clamp that fits onto the can or even a tray for a roller.

Photograph courtesy of W. L. Sims.

If rubber-base paint has been used, the caustic soda treatment may not be effective and it may be necessary to use an organic solvent type of paint remover.

Caution:—When using caustic soda or lye, avoid splashing eyes, skin, and clothing.

Interior Metal

Interior metal, such as heating grilles, radiators, and exposed water pipes, should be painted to prevent rust and to make them as inconspicuous as possible. New metal should be cleaned of grease and dirt by washing with mineral spirits, and any rust should be removed by sanding, after which a metal primer should be applied. The finish coat may be either a flat wall paint or a semi-gloss enamel.

If you are not sure of the primer to use on metal, the paint dealer or manufacturer will give you this

There are many gadgets besides a steady painting hand to avoid getting paint on glass when you paint the windows. An old but still reliable technique is to coat the glass with a soap-and-water "paste." When the job is over, just wash the windows and the paint smears come right off with soap. But wait until the paint is dry before you wash the soap off.

If you have tileboard made of hardboard in your home and you want "mortar" lines, you can paint them in. An easy way to do this is with a striping tool; it comes with various wheels, depending upon the width of line you wish to paint.

Photograph courtesy of Masonite Corp.

information, dependent on the type of metal to be painted.

Usually on exposed air ducts of galvanized metal a primer coat of zinc dust-zinc oxide paint is used, before the finish coat is applied.

The paints may be applied by brush or spray; the small spray attachment for vacuum cleaners is very convenient, especially for painting radiators.

Brass lighting fixtures and andirons may be polished and kept bright by coating with metal lacquers. The lacquers, held in cans under pressure, may be sprayed directly from the container. Old-fashioned or unattractive lighting fixtures may be painted with ceiling or wall paint to harmonize with the surrounding surfaces.

Special Surfaces
WHITEWASH

Whitewashes and lime paints must be thin when applied. In fact, best results will be obtained if the application is so thin that the surface to which it is applied may easily be seen through the film while it is wet. The coating will dry opaque, but two thin coats will give better results than one thick coat.

A large whitewash brush is best for applying the wash. One should not attempt to brush out the coating, as in applying oil paint, but simply spread the whitewash on as evenly and quickly as possible.

The principal ingredient in whitewash is lime paste. A satisfactory paste can be made with hydrated lime, but better results are obtained by using quicklime paste that has been slaked with enough

water to make it moderately stiff. The lime paste should be kept in a loosely covered container for at least several days. Eight gallons of stiff lime paste can be made by slaking 25 lbs. of quicklime in 10 gallons of water, or by soaking 50 lbs. of hydrated lime in 6 gallons of water. After soaking, the paste should be strained through a fine screen to remove lumps or foreign matter.

Whitewash can be made from various combinations of lime paste and other ingredients. The following two formulas are satisfactory.

Formula No. 1

Casein	5 lbs.
Trisodium phosphate	3 lbs.
Lime paste	8 gals.

Before applying any paint—either undercoat or final coat—to a wall surface, wash it thoroughly to remove all dust and grease. Otherwise, you are bound to wind up with a "paint failure."

Photograph courtesy of Pittsburgh Plate Glass.

When painting an entire room, start your painting job with the ceiling. When painting a ceiling always work across the narrow dimension.

Cracks in plaster walls should be filled before starting to paint. See **Plaster** section for detailed how-to.

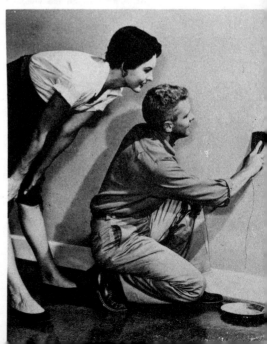

When painting a wall, keep painting strips on wall narrow so that you are always working with a wet edge. Otherwise, you may see the "joints" where new brush strokes are laid on.

Photograph courtesy of Pittsburgh Plate Glass.

Paint shields are helpful in keeping paint off the glass when painting the window sash.

The casein, which serves as the glue binder, should be soaked in 2 gallons of hot water until thoroughly softened, which should be approximately 2 hours. After dissolving the trisodium phosphate in 1 gallon of water it should be added to the casein, stirring the mixture until the casein dissolves. This solution should be mixed with the lime paste and 3 gallons of water.

Formula No. 2

Common salt ...... 12 lbs.
Powdered alum .... 6 lbs.
Molasses .... 1 qt.
Lime paste .... 8 gals.

The salt and alum should be dissolved in 4 gallons of hot water, after which the molasses may be added to the mixture. The resulting clear solution is then added to the lime paste, stirred vigorously, and thinned with water to the desired consistency. This whitewash has a yellow tinge when first applied, but the color disappears in a few days leaving a white film.

Another satisfactory whitewash can be made by diluting a moderately heavy cold lime paste (about 33 lbs. of hydrated lime and 8 gallons of water) with 5 gallons of skim-milk.

The area covered by a gallon of whitewash depends upon the nature of the surface, but ordinarily a gallon will cover about 225 sq. ft. on wood, about 180 sq. ft. on brick, and about 270 sq. ft. on plaster. The formulas mentioned will make from 10 to 14 gallons of whitewash. If a smaller quantity is desired, the amount of each ingredient should be reduced proportionately.

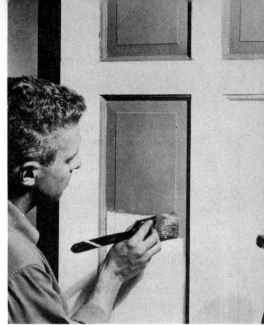

A paint shield also comes in handy when painting the baseboard molding or the bottom of a door. It protects the floor from splashes.

If painting the panels with enamel, smooth the surface with light, upward strokes, using a brush that is almost dry.

When painting a panel door, always paint the insides of the panels first with horizontal strokes.

STIPPLING

Whether you desire the effect of stippling (tiny paint dots) as a decorative effect, or if you have a wall which has an uneven surface and you feel you can hide the defect by stippling it, you may accomplish this result very simply.

For stippling you need a special brush; get one that is flat, and has short, stiff bristles.

The first step is to cover the surface with a coat of paint, using your regular paint brush, or spray, or roller. Then, while the surface is still wet, take the dry stipple brush and energetically with short strokes drive the ends or the bristles into the wet paint. Be sure not to brush across. The result will be clusters of dots. Every few minutes wipe the brush with a cloth, to keep the bristle ends clean and dry.

STENCILING

You may want designs on the walls, or perhaps even on floors and ceilings, in some of the rooms or hallway. You may buy or make your own stencils, which should be on heavy paper, stencil board, plastic, or metal. Avoid stencils made of lightweight paper which will get soaked when touched by wet paint. Your paint dealer will suggest the best paint for you to use, as it will depend a great deal on the surface over which you want to put the stencilled designs. Generally a heavy paint is used, so that it will not spread under the stencil while you are applying it.

The stencil must be held very firmly against the surface with one hand, and the stencil brush worked over it quickly with the other hand. Or, if you have an assistant, it is best for one person to keep the stencil steady, while the other does the painting. In removing the stencil, make sure you pick it up without smudging.

Painting—Miscellaneous Surfaces

Awnings and Deck Chairs

Faded or discolored awnings where the canvas is in good condition may be freshened by coating with awning paints which are available at most paint and hardware stores in a variety of nonfading colors. These materials are easily applied with a brush, are nonpenetrating, and dry to a smooth flat flexible finish. They may also be used to renew the color of old canvas on deck chairs, lawn umbrellas, or glider cushions.

Porch Decks

Exposed canvas porch decks are difficult to maintain, but may be painted with porch and deck enamel or aluminum paint. The coating should be renewed annually if the deck is to remain leakproof. Porch and deck enamel produces a glossy finish; and aluminum paint a silvery metallic finish.

Doors

In painting a door, the type of wood, the severity of exposure, the finish and color desired, and the type of paint should all be taken into consideration. When applying each coat of paint, finish the panels first, the center rail next, then the top and bottom rails, next the vertical stiles, and finally the edges. If the surface is kept smooth by rubbing with sandpaper between each coat, the door should present a smooth velvetlike appearance when finished.

Windows

Before painting a window sash, be sure to scrape off all the old, loose putty and coat the wood recesses with linseeed oil before applying the new putty. A shield cut from a piece of tin will speed the work of painting by protecting the glass from "run overs" while still permitting enough

How to Glaze and Paint Wood Sash

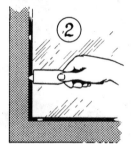

After removal of cracked glass and old putty, coat rabbet (groove) with boiled linseed oil. Let dry.

Place ribbon of putty in rabbet. Bed glass firmly against putty. Then fasten with glazing points.

Next, apply ribbon of putty to glass; smooth with putty knife. Let it set for a few weeks before painting.

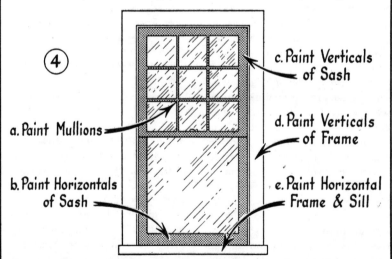

④

a. Paint Mullions

b. Paint Horizontals of Sash

c. Paint Verticals of Sash

d. Paint Verticals of Frame

e. Paint Horizontal Frame & Sill

Painting window sash is not at all difficult. Apply the paint with a small varnish brush or a flat or oval sash tool. Start with the mullions and continue as the arrows indicate. If there are paint spatters on the glass when you have finished, remove them with a razor blade soon after the paint dries.

paint to flow on to the muntins or sash bars to give a good seal between the wood and glass. The muntins or sash bars should be painted first, then the stiles and rails of the sash, next the window frames and trim and, finally, the sill and apron below.

Screens

Door and window screens will last longer and look better if kept well painted. For this, special screen paints are best, but they should be thinned to avoid clogging the mesh. A coat of thinned white paint applied to the screen wire makes the interior of the house less visible from the outside.

The necessary tools and materials are a screen paint applicator and bristle brush; special screen paint, spar varnish, or enamel in desired color and small amount of boiled linseed oil or turpentine for thinning.

A cheap grade of screen wire will probably require painting every year, while galvanized wire may show signs of rust only after long use and may then require only a light coat of paint. Copper or bronze screen wire will not deteriorate if not painted, but the corrosion products resulting from weathering make it advisable either to paint or varnish copper or bronze screens to avoid staining the trim and outside walls of a house. If it is desirable to retain the original copper or bronze color of the screens, a high-grade spar varnish should be applied in two coats to both sides of the screen cloth. Inasmuch as this will not last as long as the enamel, the screens

A life-saver for worn and scuffed articles made of leather or leatherette is a special flexible paint. It is brushed on like lacquer and dries in a few minutes to form a durable, non-bleeding film as flexible and natural-looking as the leather itself. It comes in a variety of colors for use on upholstery, luggage, convertible tops, awnings and boat decks.

Photograph courtesy of Wayne Products Co.

will need to be coated with spar varnish at least every other season. If a dark color is not objectionable, a coat of black enamel should last several seasons.

Paint may be applied evenly and economically to screens with a special screen applicator. Most paint dealers carry these applicators but, if not available, they are not difficult to make. A block of wood 1"x3"x8" may be covered with thick felt or carpet attached to the face side of the block with the nap outward. A cleat of wood for a handle should be

nailed along the center of the opposite side of the block. The carpet may be fastened by glue or tacks but if tacks or brads are used, the heads should be well embedded so that they will not catch on the wire mesh while the paint is being applied.

The screen should be placed on a level surface like a table top, and cleaned of all dust, soot, and loose rust with a bristle brush. If more thorough cleaning is necessary, the screen may be washed with soap and warm water applied with a brush, rinsed with clear water, and dried with a cloth. After the screen has been cleaned on both sides and dried thoroughly, paint may be applied by brushing the face of the applicator with a moderate amount of paint and spreading the paint over the screen with the applicator. In this way, the screen may be painted quite rapidly and easily with a thin even coating without clogging the mesh.

The frames should not require painting oftener than once in every 3 to 5 years. If the screening is cleaned and painted once a year as described, its life will be prolonged and the screens will present a neat appearance.

Swimming Pools

Vitreous tile is the preferred coating for swimming pool wall and floor surfaces, but there are three general types of paint which may be used as decorative finishes: Cement-water paints, enamel paints with water-resisting varnish vehicle, and waterproof enamel paints. These paints are available in appropriate light blue and light green colors.

The advantages of cement-water paints are their ease of application and low cost; their disadvantages are their tendency to absorb body oils and grease and to accumulate algae when it exists. One season is the maximum period that wall and floor surfaces of a much-used pool coated with cement-water paints can be kept in good condition without repainting.

Enamel paints must be applied only to clean surfaces and no water should be put into the pool for several days after the application of each coat. Enamel paints give a smooth attractive surface that may last for a season, but may develop blisters and peel during that time.

A deep luster can be obtained and the color of the wood preserved by applying a protective surface coat over either interior or exterior wood furniture. This final coat can be brushed on or, if you have the equipment, sprayed on.

Photograph courtesy of Monsanto Chemical Co.

Waterproof enamel paints will probably give the least trouble since they dry to a smooth hard-gloss finish and are chemically resistant to moisture and water-purifying agents.

Wood Furniture

For information on various finishes—refer to the section on *Furniture Finishing.*

Baby Furniture

Furniture with which the baby comes into contact must be finished with a non-poisonous paint, especially if the child has a tendency to lick, taste, and chew everything within reach. Buy special baby enamel, which comes in pretty colors and is washable. This applies to painted toys, too.

Fiber Rug

This may be painted with canvas or awning paint. See the section on *Fiber Rug, Painting.*

Painting— Technique of Spraying

Applying paint with a sprayer is faster than with either a brush or a roller, but you'll need more experience in handling this "tool" than either the brush or roller to produce a satisfactory job.

Spray painting can be done in a variety of ways:

1. You can use the simple spray attachment that usually comes with a vacuum cleaner, particularly the tank type cleaner. However, the air pressure is low and this type of sprayer works best on thin liquids. This sprayer has an elementary control and is not suitable for fine lacquer or precision spraying.

2. You can purchase pressurized-aerosol cans with different types of paints in a variety of colors. This technique works fine for touch-

Guns having internal-mix nozzles generally have three interchangeable nozzles to produce different types of patterns. The 45° nozzle is very useful for spraying floors or ceilings, since you can paint at an angle without tipping the gun.

The overshot type of external-mix nozzles produce a round pattern, while the other external-mix nozzles produce a fan-shaped pattern. The higher-priced guns of this type usually are made with a built-in spray-pattern adjustment to vary the pattern from round to fan-shaped—the one nozzle serves all purposes.

up painting, especially on appliances. However, because of the limited amount of paint held by the pressurized can, this is a costly method for painting large areas.

3. Inexpensive vibrator-type sprayer guns are available and they are considerably better than the attachments made for vacuum cleaners. However, they vary in the quality of performance and some can-

not be used for really efficient spray painting. Others, however, are satisfactory and work well with most types of paints.

4. Sprayers of the diaphragm type or working off a compressor are the more professional tools to use for spraying. These are more expensive than the vibrator type and, on the average, perform more efficiently than the vibrator type.

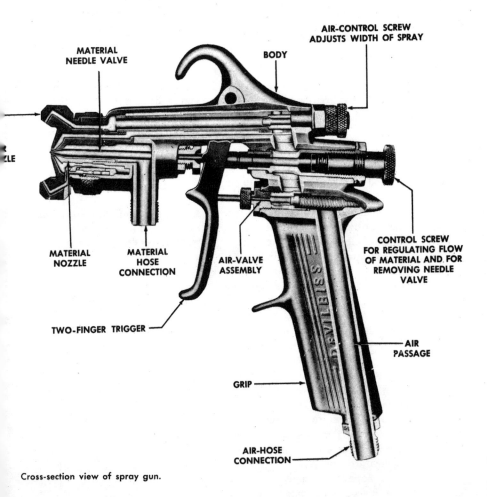

Cross-section view of spray gun.

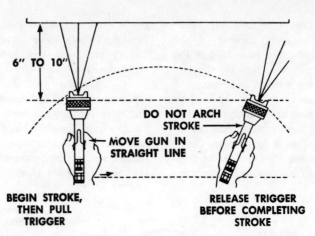

**BEGIN STROKE,
THEN PULL
TRIGGER**

**RELEASE TRIGGER
BEFORE COMPLETING
STROKE**

Proper way to spray a surface—begin the stroke and then pull the trigger, continuing to move your hand in a straight line. Release pressure on the trigger and stop spraying before you complete the stroke.

Selecting the Sprayer

You can paint about four to six times faster with a sprayer than with any other painting tool. When you select a paint sprayer, you should be guided by the following factors:

1. Capacity—how much will the sprayer hold? Can it be used with all types of paints or only certain ones?

2. What is its speed—how much paint can it deliver per minute?

3. What are its design qualities —is it convenient to handle? Is it easy to operate? Can you clean it easily? Does it have interchangeable nozzles?

While these are the primary factors to consider, you should also examine three other points governing the use of sprayers:

1. Type of air supply

• Bleeder-type guns are de-

signed for direct connection of the gun to the compressor so that the air is blowing through the sprayer at all times. The trigger action is used only to control the flow of the paint through the gun.

• Non-bleeder guns operate

Spray gun should be held perpendicular to the surface. If held at an angle, there will be an uneven deposit of paint.

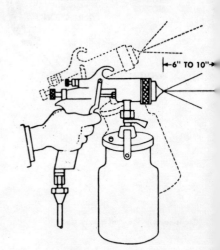

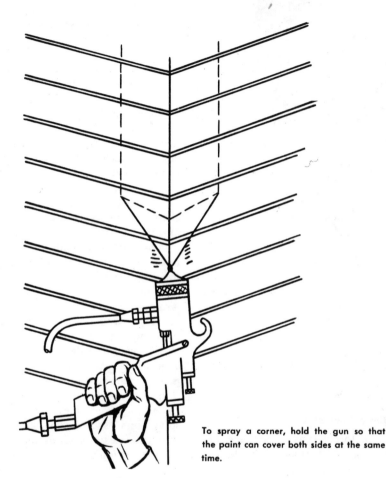

To spray a corner, hold the gun so that the paint can cover both sides at the same time.

with the trigger shutting off both the air supply and the paint. They cannot be used with continually-running compressors since shutting off the air flow at the gun would result in the bursting of the air supply line or blowing the safety valve on the compressor.

2. Paint feed to the nozzle

• Pressure-fed guns have an air-tight cup to hold the paint. Air pressure on the top of the paint forces it up to the gun nozzle.

• Syphon guns depends upon suction to lift the paint from the cup or container into the air stream at the outlet of the nozzle.

3. How the paint is atomized for spraying

• Internal-mix nozzles atomize the paint in a mixing chamber inside the nozzle. This provides for a better mixing of the heavier paints used with a spray gun.

• External-mix nozzles atomize the paint in air jets outside the noz-

It's a wise policy to wear a respirator mask whenever you paint with a spray gun.

zle. This type is best used with lighter paints and quick-drying paints which might otherwise tend to clog the nozzle.

Basic Preparation

Before starting to spray, the surface should be thoroughly cleaned and all rough spots smoothed with sandpaper and wiped free of dust. Everything in a room that might be marred by settling spray should be covered with old sheets or dropcloths.

Before starting to spray, door knobs, wall switches, and light fixtures should be covered with masking tape which can be obtained in paint and hardware stores in widths from ½″ up.

Masking tape should also be laid along the frames of windows and mirrors. The glass should be coated with masking compound which may be obtained from paint and automotive supply stores. In bathrooms, use tape and newspapers to mask tub, lavatory and toilet.

If masking is not feasible, a piece of metal or stiff cardboard may be used as a shield, moving it along as the spraying proceeds. This is a convenient way to separately spray screen wire and screen frames.

All paint materials used in a spray gun should be strained through a clean, relatively lint-free cloth before using.

TYPE OF MATERIAL	TYPE OF FEED REQUIRED			TYPE OF NOZZLE REQUIRED		
	Pressure	Syphon	Either	Internal Mix	External Mix	Either
Enamel			x			x
Lacquer			x		x	
Shellac	x				x	
Stain			x			x
Undercoat	x			x		
Water Paint			x			x
Oil Paint	x			x		
Synethetic Paint			x			x

Spray guns come in various shapes and sizes. This model with an adjustable nozzle can be used with paint in the large aluminum can or with a special plastic hose to draw the liquid out of a large drum so that there is no stopping for refilling.

Photograph courtesy of Champion Sprayer.

Spraying With a Gun

When spraying paint, always wear a respirator. It gives valuable protection against paint poisoning and should be worn even for outdoor work with a cap to keep drift

Touch-up painting is easy with a pressurized spray can. Here, lacquer is used to refinish a lamppost outside the home.

Photograph courtesy of Plasti-Kote, Inc.

spray out of the hair. Do not smoke while spraying. (If the respirator is worn, this will be impossible.) Also make sure that ventilation is adequate for health as well as fire safety. Never spray near an open flame, or where there is a possibility of sparks flying, as spraying mixes paint and air to an explosive proportion. When painting indoors, always have the windows open wide; never spray in a closed room unless an exhaust fan is in operation that will change the air every 3 minutes.

Before actual painting operations are started, adjust the gun and practice spraying on scrap material to obtain the proper flow of paint. Hold the gun in one hand and with the other keep the hose clear of the surface that is being sprayed. The spray tip should be held 6″ to 10″ from the surface to which the paint is being applied.

If a large panel or wall is being sprayed, begin at the upper corner and work from right to left. Move down as each swath is laid on. Since the center half of the last sprayed

Enamel can also be sprayed out of a pressurized spray can to touch up rusted metal work outside the home.

Even the baby buggy can be put into trim shape with "canned" paint. The spray is fine enough to cover only a limited area so that no masking is required. Pressurized spray cans make it easy to reach out-of-the-way places.

Photographs courtesy of Plasti-Kote, Inc.

strip gets the thickest coat, lap the upper fourth of each new stroke over the lower fourth of the preceding stroke.

On each stroke, begin swinging the gun from a point to one side of where the spray is to begin. When the starting point is reached, press the trigger and hold it until the other edge of the panel sweep is reached.

Always sweep the spray stroke so that the tip of the gun stays the same distance from the surface and so that the spray will strike at right angles. The pace of the stroke should not change. Any hesitation or halt without releasing the trigger will let too much paint pile up, and a sag or run will result.

Holding the gun too close to the work will also produce a sag or run, and holding it too far away will fog the finish and produce a dull effect. Meeting points of the surfaces, such as corners and sharp edges, are spots

that tend to catch too much paint and are sprayed best with short successive spurts, aiming the gun so that each spurt is at right angles to the nearest surface. This technique applies to any finish.

A few specific suggestions follow:

1. In spraying paint, varnish, and enamel, the material should first be thinned in accordance with the manufacturers' instructions.

2. The first coat should then be "fogged" on, holding the gun a little further from the surface than the suggested 6″ to 10″.

3. One coat of primer and one coat of finish may cover a surface, but two finish coats are better.

4. Allow the paint to dry thoroughly between coats, and on small objects a better finish is obtained if the surface is lightly sanded between coats.

Lacquers are rather thin materials which dry very rapidly. They should be applied in three to five coats, using the thinner recommended by the manufacturer. Lacquer cannot as a rule be successsfully applied over paints, varnish, or enamel.

Among the common faults in spray finishes are sags (finish laid on so thick that it flows downward in drapes); runs (longer drops streaking down, usually from sags); holidays (spots left bare); orange peeling (bumpy finish); and fogging (dull, pebbled finish usually resulting from the gun being held too far from the surface).

Paper Hanging

See *Wallpaper*.

Parallel Circuit

A circuit is said to be in parallel when there is a common feed and a common return between two or more fixtures or outlets, and each receives a separate portion of the current flow from the common feed. See *Electrical Wiring*.

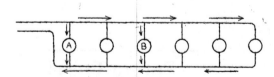

Lights and outlets in parallel.

Parallel Jaw Pliers

Some pliers are made with a special joint which permits the jaws of the pliers to remain parallel regardless of the extent of the opening. These pliers are particularly effective in holding square stock or holding parallel sides of a nut.

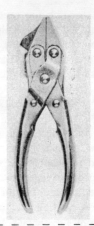

Parallel jaw pliers with wire cutter edge.

Parallels

Wedge-shaped bars, usually steel, placed with the thin end of one on the thick end of the other are used by machinists for locking work in place. The top face of the upper and the bottom face of the lower piece remain parellel. The distance between the two faces, however, can be increased or decreased by shifting one bar in relation to the other.

The home handyman can use similar bars, but made of wood, for clamping wood which has been glued until the adhesive is dry.

See *Adhesives* and *Clamps*.

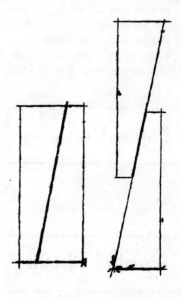

Paring Chisel and Gouge

A paring chisel is generally used with hand pressure only to make slicing cuts that are smoother surfaced than if the cuts were made directly across the grain. A gouge is similar to the chisel but has a concave face on the blade. See *Wood Turning Chisels*.

Paris Green

This is a poisonous copper arsenite mixture used not only as a pigment in painting but also as an insecticide. Its chemical formula is $CuHAsO_3$.

Parting Strip

In a double-hung window, a parting strip is a thin piece of wood used to keep the top and bottom sashes apart. See *Windows*.

Partition

No longer does room partition-ing mean a solid wall; the new and most convenient trend is the room divider, which is often merely a partial partition. For information on this subject, refer to the sections on *Room Dividers* and *Built-Ins*.

Partition Wall

Walls within the house are divided into two types—partition and bearing. Partition walls are "non-bearing"—that is, they do not bear any load as compared with a bearing wall which supports some weight. The bearing walls run at right angles to the joists above and support them.

Removing a Partition Wall

The average homeowner can remove a partition wall in his home without endangering the house structure. Removing a bearing wall, however, is a more complicated process and ordinarily should not be undertaken by the average homeowner. On the other hand, the more advanced handyman, who knows how to prop up the structure, can remove a bearing wall and replace it with a beam without endangering the house itself.

The partition wall normally runs parallel to the joist above. If you have any doubts about whether the wall is a partition or bearing wall, it is best to check with a local architect or builder. Another check you should make before attempting to remove a partition wall is for pipes running through the wall. While it is possible to shift pipes, this often involves considerable plumbing work and may be too much for the average homeowner. To remove a partition wall, you should:

1. Pry off the baseboard molding and ceiling trim on both sides of the wall.

2. Shut off the electrical power to any lines in the wall. With the fuse removed or the main switch off,

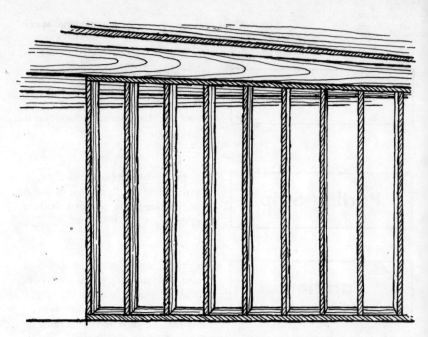

This is a bearing wall.

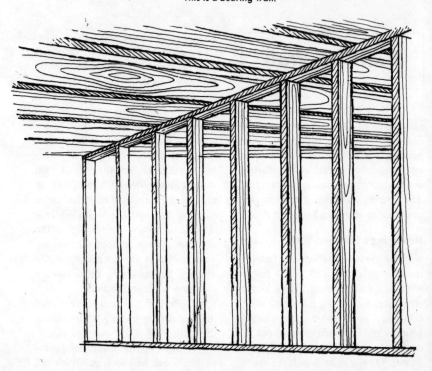

This is a partition wall.

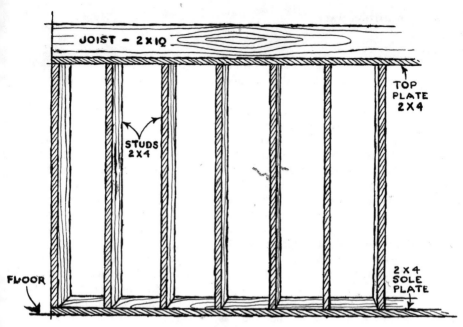

Conventional method of framing a partition wall.

Single wall material partition wall can be made of corrugated fiberglass, hardboard or plywood. Use at least ½" thickness of the latter two.

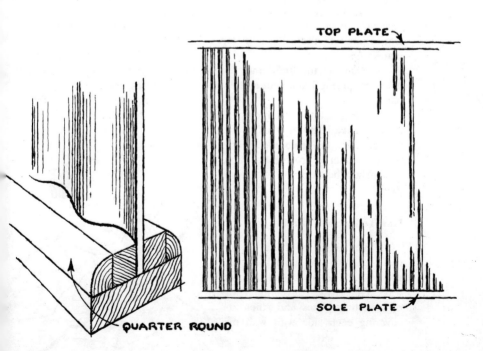

disconnect the electrical lines within the wall from either the basement or attic.

3. Break the wall material between any two studs and start to remove the old wall material. If you have plaster walls, it is necessary to chop the plaster out with a hammer and possibly a cold chisel. With wallboard, you can pry the panels loose. If you have wood walls, you may wish to remove the pieces with the least amount of damage. In that case, pry the boards loose along the sole and top plates and pull the nails out.

4. Remove the loose electrical wires from between the studs as well as any outlet boxes or wall fixture boxes.

5. To remove the studs, you may have to cut each one and pry them loose separately. In some cases, careful hammering will enable you to withdraw them uncut from between the sole and top plates.

6. Remove the sole and top plates by prying loose with a crowbar.

7. After all the partition wall sections have been removed, it will be necessary to patch the ceiling, walls and floor to provide a continuous surface between the two rooms joined.

How To Install a Partition Wall

If you wish to divide a large room into two with a partition wall, you can do so in several different ways. One is the conventional way of installing plates and studs and covering each side with wall material. However, you can use glass block, corrugated fiberglass plastic panels, or single hardboard or wood panels.

To follow the conventional method, nail a 2x3 or 2x4 sole plate to the floor and a top plate to the ceiling. Cut 2x3 or 2x4 studs to fit between the plates and toe-nail them into position. If it is necessary to add a door, see section on *Door Framing.* After the plates and studs, either 16" or 24" on center, are in place, apply the wall material to each side. To conceal the joint between the wall and floor, add a baseboard. See section on *Baseboard.* The wall-ceiling joint is also concealed with a molding; see *Ceiling Trim.* Also see *Plaster* and *Walls.*

To use a single wall material, such as corrugated fiberglass, hardboard or plywood, you can use a 1x3 for the sole and plates. The wall material is set between the plates and held in place with cleats attached to the plates on each side of the material. You can use any square stock and finish the outside edge by attaching a piece of half-round as shown in the sketch.

Patio

While the dictionary defines a patio as an enclosed court, it has come to be used to describe a terrace along side the house, a barbecue-play area with a roof, a three-wall and roofed shelter away from the house or a slab of concrete abutting the house. In many regions, the patio exists under a local name.

Here, we have used the term *patio* to describe an outdoor living area. It can be raised off the ground or flush with it. It can be sheltered with a wall or two and a roof, or exposed with but a few shrubs and trees to block the sun. It can be a sun porch, a lanai or a barbecue shelter.

Planning the Patio

Whether you are planning to build an outdoor recreation area or hope to modify your existing one, there are certain basic elements which are essential in good patio planning. One of the most important is the orientation of the patio, particularly in relation to the sun.

Merely building your patio in the back of your house so that it is sheltered from the street is a poor solution to the location problem. There are ways to have your patio face the street and yet have that needed privacy. Your first job is to decide upon the positioning of your patio in relation to the sun.

South—A patio that faces the south always has the sun, practically from sunrise to sunset. Provisions must be made to keep the sun's rays from beating down and heating the patio. A roof is a must. Some means of shielding the patio from the setting sun must also be found.

West—A patio facing the west is a hot patio for it receives the full force of the sun from early afternoon until the sun sets late in the evening during the summer. Overhead protection is a must as is some means of blocking the setting sun's rays in the late afternoon and evening.

East—Although the sun shines directly on the patio in the morning, an east patio cools off later in the day and the house blocks the sun from early afternoon on. An east patio is desirable in hot climates and, unless you wish protection from rain, there is little need for any overhead covering.

North—Facing the north, a patio receives only the very early sun and then is protected by the house for the remainder of the day. In some areas, the late setting sun may shine on the patio, but by that time the heat is gone. In other areas, where the evening turns cool, some provision for heating the outdoor living area must be provided for comfort on a north patio.

Basic Ingredients of an Attractive Patio

While orientation is of primary importance in planning a patio, there are many other factors which you should consider. No one factor makes a patio good or bad; it is a combination that does the trick. Here are some of the elements necessary to make a patio attractive and functional.

1. The patio should be oriented to invite or block out the sun, depending upon your location and

Colorful flagstone makes an attractive patio floor. Here the stones blend in with the house's exterior and the wall along the end of the patio. The sun is blocked by transluscent fiberglass roof.

Photographs courtesy of Alsynite Company of America.

Brick and redwood strips are combined to make this unusual patio floor. The path to the patio from the house is also made of brick set in sand with a ground cover used as part of the pavement pattern. The entire area is shaded by a fiberglass roof, which keeps the hot sun out but permits light to pass through.

what you require of an outdoor living area.

2. A well-planned patio is part of the house; it is not just an addition! Your patio design should blend in with your home's over-all design and architecture.

3. A "room" outdoors must .be bigger than one inside the home. Provide adequate space for the larger-sized furniture and leave plenty of space for "breathing."

4. Add to the take-it-easy atmosphere outdoors by providing comfortable furniture for dining and relaxing.

5. Your patio should blend in with your landscaping and garden planning.

6. Privacy outdoors can be gained partly by orientation of the patio and partly by the use of fences and shields.

7. Controlling the weather can be achieved by adding a roof to keep off the hot sun or to provide a sheltered area away from the wind and rain.

8. To many, a patio is not a patio without a barbecue. You can either build a barbecue as part of the patio or use a mobile unit.

9. While the adults are relaxing outdoors, it is often desirable to have the children playing nearby. Provide for a game area for the youngsters, teen-agers and adults. The play area for young children should be close enough so that they can be supervised but far enough away so that they are not disturbing.

10. Shrubs and attractive plantings help make outdoor living more attractive and relaxing.

11. With certain patios, a fireplace is needed, particularly on cooler evenings. If you live in such a locality, plan on building a fireplace as part of the outdoor living area.

12. The patio floor should be durable, easy to clean, attractive, easy to walk on, quick drying, glare free and non-skid.

13. Some provision for outdoor storage is necessary. Even with a patio built adjoining the house, it's handy to have some place outdoors to keep cooking equipment, game supplies and other outdoor items.

Patio Pavements

There are many different types of paving materials you can use for your outdoor living center. Each of the materials has its own advantages and shortcomings. Which you select will depend to some extent upon how much you wish to spend on your patio and the effect you wish to achieve.

Concrete is frequently used for it can be poured easily by the homeowner. You can color it, if you wish, and finish it in different ways, from a smooth slick surface to a pebbly surface. However, it must be laid properly or you may have difficulty later. See *Concrete*.

Flagstones are probably the most expensive of all patio paving materials. However, they cannot be matched for their performance or beauty. They are very rugged but some people find it difficult to lay them in pleasing patterns and color arrangements. See section *Patio— Flagstone*. Frequently slate is used

Which way does your patio face? West patios are hot; north patios are cold. For a decorative touch, and as a means of orientation, you can imbed an attractive brass compass in your patio pavement. These compasses come in many styles and are made of ¼" cast brass. They can be installed in any surface as they have spurs on the back for bonding.

Photograph courtesy of Manor Crafts.

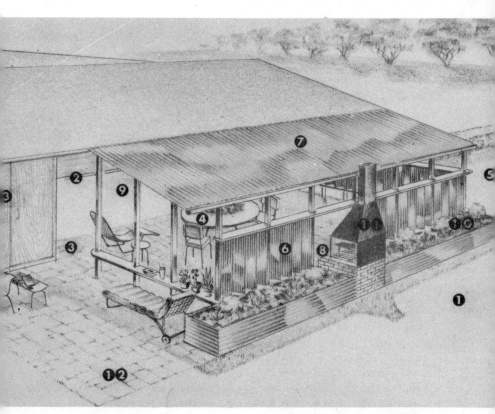

Sketch courtesy of Monsanto Chemical Co.

Pebbly-concrete combined with slick concrete produce a striking pavement for this patio. Note that the wood fence for privacy is combined with an overhead wooden frame with plastic fiberglass panels to provide necessary shade for the outdoor living area.

in place of flagstone; it is quite durable but considerably less expensive. However, it is not available in as many or as rich colors.

Bricks are also very popular and provide a pleasing, skid-proof surface. They are simple to lay and can be set either in a bed of sand or concrete, but when laid in sand, there is the possibility of their heaving during cold weather. Furthermore, they stain easily and may split under excessive weight or a sharp blow. In addition, you cannot use brick as a surface if you want an outdoor dancing area. See section *Patio— Brick*.

Concrete Blocks are available in many colors and are usually made 8″x16″ and 2″ thick. Of course, you can make your own blocks with regular or ready-mix concrete. These blocks can be laid in the same manner as brick in sand. They are as durable as concrete but, unless set on a properly laid base, they are likely to heave during cold weather.

Tiles come in a variety of colors, shapes and sizes and can be made into a very attractive patio. They are particularly effective in homes where the outdoor living area is an extension of indoor living space, separated by sliding glass doors.

Concrete with swirl lines is used for this patio floor. It blends perfectly with the house's exterior wall and the patio "flows" as part of the house. Transluscent fiberglass is used for a privacy fence and a patio roof.

Photograph courtesy of Filon Co.   Photograph courtesy of Sakrete, Inc.

Individual concrete blocks set into sand make a pleasing patio pavement. These blocks, poured by the homeowner in molds, can be colored and made in different sizes.

Patio tiles produce a slick, smooth surface for an outdoor living area. Part of this relaxation center is shielded from the sun by a fiberglass roof and privacy is obtained by tall-growing hedges.

Photograph courtesy of Alsynite Company of America.

Pavement Checklist

What should you look for when selecting a paving material for your patio? Here are several checkpoints to consider before you select the material:

1. A good paving material should be durable. It should be weather-resistant so that it doesn't melt in the hot sun or buckle or crack in the cold weather.

2. The pavement should be comfortable to walk on. It should not be hot· underfoot in the hot summer, nor should it be soft and gummy.

3. The material should harmonize with the material used for your home exterior. Pay particular attention to its texture.

4. The paving material should be easy to clean, preferably by washing off with a garden hose. Furthermore, it should not require frequent repairs.

6. The surface, al-though relatively smooth, should be glare-free and skid-proof. Soft-looking materials are usually more attractive than the hard and slick surfaces.

7. Remember price when you are selecting material. The patio usually has to be of reasonable cost. You will find that asphalt is about the cheapest while colored, matched-cut flagstones are the most expensive.

8. When building your own patio, consider the problem of material handling when selecting a paving surface. Some types of patio pavements are easy to install by yourself; others require special equipment and helping hands.

The tiles must be laid in concrete and you must be extra careful to avoid staining them with mortar as you set them in place. See *Tiles*.

Asphalt is the least expensive of all the patio paving materials. If laid properly, it can be durable. The homeowner can lay asphalt in small quantities at a time as the material comes already mixed and can be purchased at some hardware stores, building supply yards and even lumber yards. However, asphalt is affected by heat and under the hot sun it becomes soft and tacky. It is not recommended for hot patios in any section of the country.

Other Materials that can be used for patios include gravel, tanbark, crushed brick, adobe block and even compacted sand. Look all the materials over and then make your choice of the material best suited for your needs.

Patio—Blocks

Making your own "flagstones" out of concrete can be done in your spare time. You can pour these blocks in molds in your basement or garage during rainy weather or during the winter so that you can lay your patio quickly once you are set to work outdoors.

These blocks can be made in different sizes and shapes and, if you wish, you can color some to achieve a colored flagstone effect at a considerably lower price. While it is possible to mix a batch of concrete for each mold, you will probably find it more convenient and cleaner too, if you use a ready-mixed preparation. All you have to do is add water to the mix and then pour it into the mold.

For the best results, the blocks should be laid on a sand base or firmly compacted, well-drained soil. If you have a clay-like soil, remove the upper 3″ to 4″ and pour sand into the area which the blocks will cover. Wet it down and compact it with a lawn roller. In this way, there is less likelihood of the blocks heaving during the winter when water under the blocks freezes and expands.

Working with Concrete "Flagstones"

In addition to the concrete "flagstones," shown in this series of step-by-step photographs, you can prepare other types of forms to

1. Lay out the area for the patio or terrace by hammering stakes into the ground and connecting them with string. You will be able to get an idea as to the size and shape of your outdoor living area.

4. You need only ordinary hand tools to make the form for the blocks. Use a hand saw to cut the pieces of 2x2 to size, to form make 2′x2′ with notches so you can make 1′x2′ blocks as well.

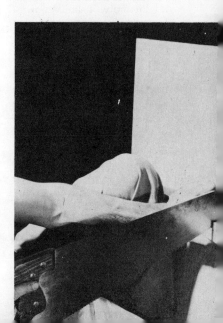

2. Draw a sketch of your proposed patio to scale on a large sheet of paper. Then you can mark off the individual concrete blocks and even color them to see how the finished job will look.

3. The form for the individual concrete blocks is made of 2x2 stock. Note that notches or dadoes are cut in the individual piesces so that they can be fitted together to make the form.

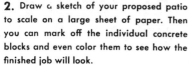

Photographs courtesy of Sakrete, Inc.

5. A mallet and chisel are the only other tools needed besides the saw. Use the mallet and chisel to knock out the piece of wood cut on each side by the saw to form the notch.

6. The form is fitted together; no nails are used in order to make it easy to take form apart after block has cured. Keep a piece of metal or hardboard under the form.

7. The cement for the concrete blocks can be mixed in any convenient place. Here a wheelbarrow is being used, but you can even mix it on the basement or garage floor.

8. Measure the water carefully. If you wish to color the blocks, add the pigments before adding the water. For coloring techniques, see section on **Concrete**.

11. To round or form the corners of the stones, use an edger. This masonry tool is available at most hardware stores and costs little. It makes for a professional-looking job.

12. After the edges has been formed, trowel the top surface smooth. A steel trowel is used to produce a slick, smooth surface; a wood float will produce a coarser surface.

9. Mix the concrete (Portland cement, sand and gravel) thoroughly to the proper consistency. You can do this with a garden hoe or even the shovel or spade used for measuring.

10. Pour the concrete into the form with a shovel. Take a convenient length of 1x2 or 1x3 and use it as a "strike board" to level off the concrete flush with the top of the form.

13. Prepare the base for the concrete block patio by laying at least 2" of fine, clean sand over well-drained, compact soil. Level out the sand and begin to set blocks in place according to your plan.

14. Set each concrete block in place carefully leaving about ½" to 1" space between the blocks to form the "mortar" lines. Check now and then to make certain that all blocks are level.

15. To fill the spaces between the blocks, pour some sand over the finished area and with a wide broom, brush the sand over the blocks and into the openings.

Photographs courtesy of **Sakrete, Inc.**

16. Note how the sand flows into the dividing spaces between the blocks. You can finish one section at a time or lay all the blocks and then fill the openings between them with sand.

make the stones in different shapes. On page 2099 are several typical patterns together with the word form details.

It is best to use 2x2 lumber for the forms and cut them to the size and shape as noted in the diagrams. In order to avoid cracking the concrete after it has cured, it is best to make the forms with notches or dadoes so that the form can be taken apart easily and the flagstone removed. Where separation strips are called for in the diagrams of the blocks, you can use 1x2 or 2x2 lumber, cutting notches, where possible.

If you wish, you can use the separation strips without notches. Merely set them into place inside the form and hold them in position with double-headed nails set through the form into the strips. Later, when you are ready to remove the flagstones, you can withdraw the double-headed nails easily and remove the outside frame held together with interlocking notches.

Before you undertake this project, it is best to read the section in an earlier volume on *Concrete*. Once you have learned how to mix and pour concrete properly, you will find it smooth sailing for the rest of the project.

While you can color individual blocks (see the coloring how-to in the section on *Concrete*), you may wish to leave all the blocks in their natural color and use fine, crushed gravel to fill the spaces between the blocks. On the other hand, you may wish to set the blocks onto a concrete base and fill the openings between the blocks with colored concrete.

There are many variations you can use when making this striking concrete block patio. Explore the different possibilities before you touch the concrete. Plan carefully in advance and you will find that here is a patio that you can make yourself quickly, easily and inexpensively. What's more, you and your family can have lots of fun in planning, building and living on it.

It is possible to make a number of large-size concrete blocks, practically 30″ squares as used for sidewalks, and have an attractive outdoor living center for entertaining the family and guests.

Photograph courtesy of Reynolds Metals Co.

Three typical patterns you can use when making your own flagstones or tiles out of concrete. Always set the forms on a sheet of metal, hardboard or exterior grade of plywood.

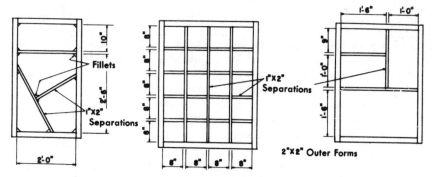

TYPICAL PATTERNS

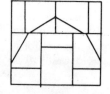
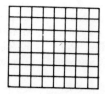

Patio—Brick

A brick patio is one of the easiest for the homeowner to make. Furthermore, it provides a pleasing, inviting surface which can be yours with only a moderate expenditure. During the cold winter when the garden is dead and drab, the touch of red is a welcome sight.

You can make a patio of this type with either new or used brick. Whether you use face brick, decorative brick or colored brick blocks, you will be able to produce a striking addition for your outdoor living area. Should you prefer a color other than red or gray-white, both standard for brick, you may wish to paint your patio brick. You can do the job easily with a long-nap roller. See the section on *Painting*. You'd be surprised at the unusual effects you can create by painting your brick patio.

A brick patio can be built a section at a time. At some time in the future, if you should wish to enlarge your outdoor living area, it's easy to add extra brick. If you wish to change the shape or position of your patio, just pick up the bricks and set them down in the new location. Mixing humus and top soil in with the sand will prepare the soil for a lawn or shrubs; it's as easy as that!

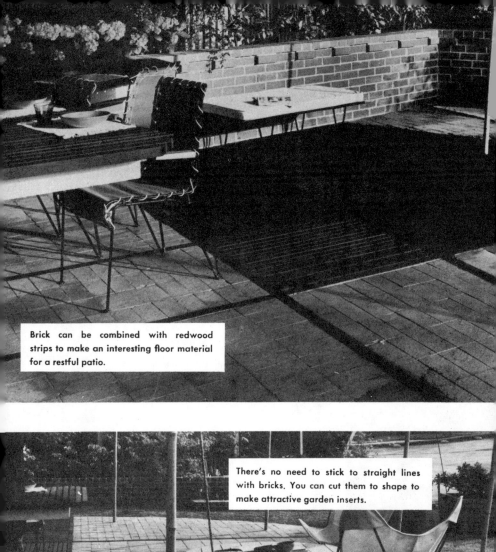

Brick can be combined with redwood strips to make an interesting floor material for a restful patio.

There's no need to stick to straight lines with bricks. You can cut them to shape to make attractive garden inserts.

Laying a Brick and Sand Patio

1. Dig out the top 2" of the area to be occupied by the patio if you have compact, well-drained soil. Set 1x4's along perimeter using 1x2's as stakes every 3' to 4'. Fill within 2¼" of top with sand.

2. Bricks for the outside border are set on end in holes dug through the sand and soil below. Top of the bricks should be flush with top of the 1x4's set along the perimeter of the patio.

3. Level the sand within the patio area. You can do this with a 36" board attached to your garden rake. Compact the sand with a roller; then wet the sand. A week later, roll the sand again.

4. Use a level guide line to lay the brick. Tie a piece of string around two bricks set at opposite ends of the patio; check levelness of several spots. If sand is too high, remove some; add sand if the level is too low.

5. Now lay the brick in the pattern you have selected. Start at any corner and work across the narrower dimension. Set bricks as close together as possible but keep the spacing between bricks even.

6. After all the bricks have been set into place, pour some sand on the surface. Use a broom or brush to sweep the sand into the openings between the bricks until the sand is flush with the top surface.

SOIL

1

BRICKS ON END

2

LAWN ROLLER

3

4

BRICK **STRING**

5

6

Patterns With Brick

Basket weave

Variations in Brick

Bricks can be laid in many handsome patterns. You can line the bricks up in evenly-spaced rows but, with a little experimentation, you will find a large number of patterns you can make.

Set in a basket-weave pattern or in square herringbone, you can create a very formal outdoor living area. On the other hand, a diagonal herringbone or a combination of wood and brick can be used to create an informal outdoor living area.

Try your hand at some of these combinations! Before you set the bricks in place, take a number of them to a clear area and set out different patterns. See how they blend in with your exterior surroundings. Try several before you select one so that you will be sure you have the best one for your purpose.

Edge treatments vary. You can use the technique of setting the brick on edge along the perimeter as shown on the preceding pages or you can follow the same method but set the brick in a bed of concrete. Or, you can use a wood board

Running bond

Diagonal herringbone

Square herringbone

End-lined

Column and row combination

to hold the perimeter of the patio. Bricks, laid on their flat side, do not make a durable edge for a brick patio. They are too apt to shift in position or chip or crack under pressure.

Brick-in-concrete edge can be made by digging out a trench about 8″ below the ground level and about 4″ wide. Pour about 2″ of concrete into the bottom of this trench. Then set the brick in place on its edge so that the top end of the brick is level with the top of the patio. Continue to add bricks and concrete on both sides of the bricks until the concrete is flush with ground level. Let this border set for several days to cure. Then proceed with the patio, laying it in the manner previously described.

A wood edge is easy to install. It is best to use redwood, which is naturally weather- and decay-resistant. Cedar is good too. While any lumber can be used, it is necessary to protect it with a wood preservative. Use 1x4 boards and set stakes, usually 1x2's, every 4′ along the outside edge of the board. The stakes should be about 16″ long and set into the ground so that the top of the stake is flush with the 1x4. After the patio is in place, the grass will grow up to the border and conceal the stakes.

Wood can be combined with bricks to form an inviting patio. It is best to use redwood or cedar for they will last longer. You can use 1x4's set into the sand so that the top of the boards is flush with the top of the bricks, or 2x3's laid on their narrow side, so that a flat surface with the brick results.

Patio—Concrete

Photograph courtesy of National Cotton Council.

A concrete patio can be as simple or as decorative as you wish to make it. The homeowner can mix and pour his own concrete or he can prepare the patio area, making the necessary forms and then have a transit-mix company bring the mixed concrete to his door.

Many homeowners prefer concrete because it is exceedingly durable and comparatively inexpensive. It does have a "cold" look so that some special treatment is necessary to make a concrete patio inviting.

Making a concrete patio is virtually the same as making a concrete sidewalk—only the area covered is larger. Here's the how-to:

1. The first step is to mark off the ground where the patio is to be laid, using stakes and string to outline the area.

2. Dig out the area to a depth of about 10″ to prevent heaving during cold weather. If you live in an area where frost is relatively unimportant, a depth of 3″ to 4″ will be sufficient.

3. If you have dug to the 10″ level, fill the bottom 6″ with cinders, gravel or crushed stone. This will form a solid base for the concrete and prevent cracking and crumbling during freezing weather.

4. Use 2x4 or 2x6 boards to outline the perimeter of the patio. Support these by 2x4 stakes driven into the ground on the outside of the concrete area.

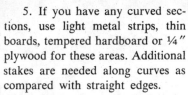

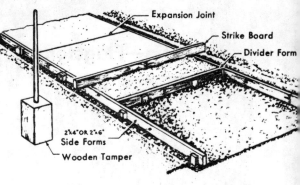

5. If you have any curved sections, use light metal strips, thin boards, tempered hardboard or ¼" plywood for these areas. Additional stakes are needed along curves as compared with straight edges.

6. Grade the patio so that the water runs away from the house. It is necessary to check all the boards alnog the perimeter to see that there is a gentle slope away from the house.

7. Set a 1x4 along the perimeter where the concrete patio will butt up against the house or any other large concrete area. Also set division boards, 1x4, at intervals of about 6'.

8. Actual pouring of the concrete is next. But before you pour, make certain that the fill is compact. Whether you mix your own concrete, purchase ready-mixed concrete or transit mix, make certain that you are using the right proporton of cement, sand and gravel. For full concrete how-to see the section on *Concrete*.

9. Level the concrete with a strike board; any board, such as a 1x4 or 1x6 that's big enough to reach from one side to the other side of the patio, will do.

Details for pouring concrete are the same for a patio as for a sidewalk—only the area is larger.

10. At intervals of about 20', expansion joints should be inserted. You can buy ready-made expansion strips or else place a 1x4, which is removed after the concrete is cured; the opening is filled with asphalt.

11. Trowel the surface smooth with a wood or steel float and finish the edges with an edger. If a rough, gritty surface is desired, finish the surface with a brush or broom.

Smooth the surface with a steel or wood float, depending upon whether you want a smooth surface or a textured surface.

Sketch and photograph courtesy of
Sakrete, Inc.

Patio—Flagstone

For unmatched natural beauty, nothing surpasses multi-colored flagstone. Whether irregular-cut or rectangular-cut, natural flagstone produces a rich-looking patio or terrace. The stones are exceedingly rugged and, if properly laid, will survive the most severe winter weather. It is possible to use slate in place of flagstone and obtain an attractive patio at considerably lower cost.

To build a flagstone patio, it is necessary to have a concrete base or foundation. A footing, about 12" deep and 8" wide, is necessary along the perimeter of the patio.

Dig out the area of the patio to a depth of 6" plus the thickness of the flagstone in areas where a firm foundation is required. In other sections, with well-drained, compact soil, excavate to a depth of 3" plus the thickness of the flagstone.

Fill the excavated portion with cinders, crushed stone or gravel to within 2" plus the flagstone thickness from the top. Then pour a concrete mix over the remaining 2". See section on *Concrete*. It is necessary to let the concrete cure before you can proceed to lay the flagstones.

You can buy flagstones cut in irregular shapes or cut, keyed and matched, depending upon how much you wish to spend. See the accompanying sketches on the next page for patterns of flagstone.

After the concrete has cured, you can lay the flagstones. It is best to set small sections of the stones in place on top of the concrete to check the pattern and color match of the tiles. In this way, you can fit the pieces together better, unless you have purchased stones that have

been cut to fit together and are keyed or marked for exact placement.

Once the stones are in position and you are satisfied with the pattern, pick up the stones but keep them in the proper position. Now, apply a thin coat of cement (1 part Portland cement to 2½ parts clean fine sand) over the concrete and set the flagstones in place. Keep the spaces between even.

After the stones have been positioned, use the same cement mix and fill the space between the stones so that the mortar joint is practically flush with the top of the stones. Use a pointing trowel or pipe to finish the mortar joints. For howto, see discussion on pointing in section on *Bricks*.

1. Make a 1:2:4 mix (1 part Portland cement, 2 parts clean sand and 4 parts gravel) for the footing and foundation of the flagstone patio. Mix all ingredients thoroughly while dry and then add the proper amount of water. Pour footing and foundation, leveling the foundation with a strike board. Let this cure before you add the flagstones.

2. After you have decided upon the exact placement of individual stones, spread a cement mix of 1 part Portland cement to 2½ parts clean sand over the concrete base and set stones in place. Do a small section at a time. Periodically, test to see that the stones are level by using a long board and a level.

3. Fill the spaces between the flagstones with the same cement mix. It is a good idea to apply several coats of floor wax to the top surfaces of the stones before you set them in the cement or place any cement between them. This wax surface protects the stones from staining by the cement; furthermore, it adds to their luster.

Irregular

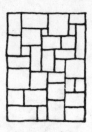
Rectangular

Semi-Rectangular

European

Paving Designs for Natural Flag-stone Patios

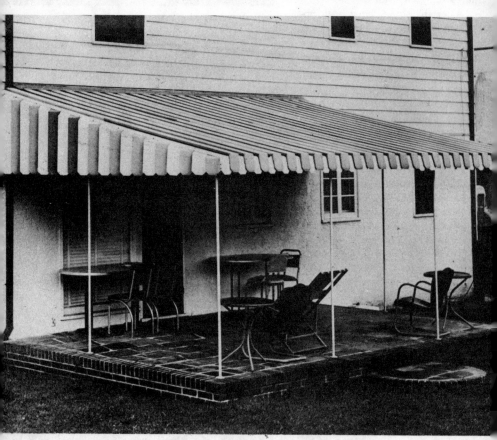

Raised terrace has bricks along the perimeter. See sections on **Brick** and **Foundation** for how-to details.

You can add to the beauty of your flagstone patio or terrace by making the walks out of flagstone too. It is necessary to pour concrete for the walk to within 1½" of the top level of the proposed walk. If you need steps, use wood forms, as shown, to pour the individual steps. When the concrete has cured, spread a thin layer of cement over it and set the stones in place as you would for a patio or terrace. For additional information on handling the stones, see section on **Flagstone**.

Patio—Tiles

Traditional burned clay tile, in its warm red color, enhances the patio or terrace. Patio tile may be laid directly on the ground or on a concrete base. It can also be laid over wood floors, porches and steps.

The easiest method of installing patio tile is to lay it on tamped ground with a leveled bed of sand, ¼″ or more in thickness. The tiles are spaced to leave a joint which can be filled with sand or moss, just as brick set in sand.

For a more permanent job, it is advisable to set the tile in a bed of cement mortar ¾″ to 1½″ thick and to leave an average ¾″ joint between the tiles to be filled with cement mortar. This, in colder climates, has to be built on a foundation similar to that used for a flagstone patio, described previously.

Of course, proper drainage must be provided for, especially if the area is large. This can be done by sloping the entire area gently toward one edge or end, along which a shallow drain gutter or ditch can be placed. Or one or more drain basins can be installed with the area pitched toward the drain. A minimum slope of ⅛″ per 1′ is recommended.

If you wish to cover an unpaved porch which is at ground level, the concrete foundation walls around the outer edges should be brought up within 2½″ of the desired finished porch level. The area within the foundation walls should be filled with earth, tamped and graded. The tile are then laid on a 1½″ mortar setting bed placed over the tamped earth and reinforced with chicken wire mesh in the mortar.

If the tiles are to be laid over an existing wood porch floor, it is necessary to cover the wood with heavy waterproof building paper. A stucco or chicken wire mesh should be stretched tightly and nailed in place ¼″ above the paper. You can use fiber washers to raise the mesh that ¼″. The tile should be imbedded in ⅞″ or more of mortar on the top of the wire mesh. The mortar thickness should not be more than ⅞″ if the wood structure is not strongly built, for patio tile on 1″ of mortar weighs 20 pounds per square foot.

Patio tile, such as that produced by Kraftile, comes in a number of sizes and shapes. They are made in 6″x6″, 6″x12″, 12″x12″

1. Remove dirt to a depth of 3″ below surface level of patio. Area to be covered should be finished off reasonably smooth and level. (This makes the right depth for 2″ sand and ⅞″ of tile.)

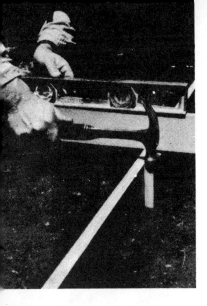

2. Install 1x3 form boards (dressed lumber) around area. First drive stakes approximately 3' apart. Nail on form boards even with top of stakes. Tap down on stakes until form boards are level and ¾" below desired surface level of patio.

3. Fill entire area to the top of form boards with dry sand. As an example, a patio area of 100 sq. ft. will take 17 cubic feet of sand.

Photographs courtesy of Kraftile Co.

plus 6"x12" and 12"x12" with bull-nose outside corners. These bull-nose tile have a rounded edge and are used at the outside of the patio;

the tile can then be set above the adjoining floor, and there is little danger of tripping over the square edge.

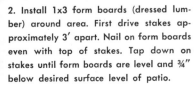

4. Screed the surface of the sand smooth and level with a straight-edged board. Slide board forward with zig-zag motion.

5. For each 100 sq. ft. of area, distribute 2 sacks of dry cement as evenly as possible over the top of the sand.

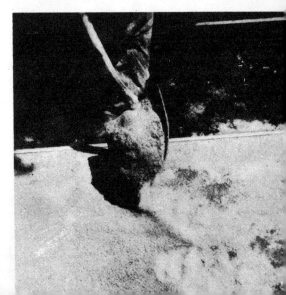

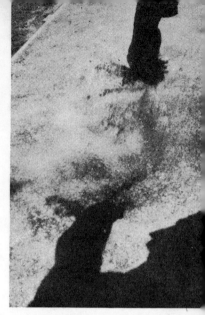

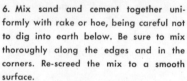

6. Mix sand and cement together uniformly with rake or hoe, being careful not to dig into earth below. Be sure to mix thoroughly along the edges and in the corners. Re-screed the mix to a smooth surface.

7. Sprinkle or "dust" pure dry cement over the smoothed surface until it is evenly covered. Use ½ sack per 100 square feet.

8. Lay dry Kraftile Patio Tile in the prepared surface. Align tiles with open joints approximately ¾" in width. For narrow joints, a piece of lath, on edge, can be used as a spacer. Lightweight Kraftile is easy to handle, edges are straight and square.

9. Check tiles for level surface. If a professional type level is not available, use your straight-edge board for this purpose, too. You'll find the smooth, flat surfaces of Kraftile make levelling easy.

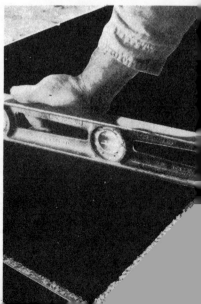

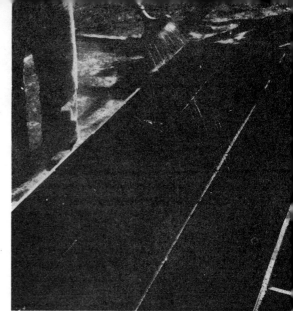

10. To set tile firmly, use a wood block for cushion and tap lightly in the center of each tile. This helps "bed" the tile.

11. Sprinkle lightly with a fine spray over the entire tile area, working back and forth and repeating until water rises to top edge of form boards. Allow to set for 24 hours.

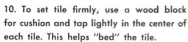

12. Prepare a grout mixture of 3 parts sand to one part cement. For 100 sq. ft. use 100 lbs. sand (1 cu. ft.) and 33 lbs. cement ($\frac{1}{3}$ cu. ft.) Add water until mix is easy to pour (like pancake batter). Pour a bead of grout to fill all joints. Stir while pouring to prevent coarser sand from settling. Let set 15 minutes.

13. A smooth struck joint is obtained by removing excess grout and smoothing with flat of trowel. For a tooled joint (shown above) bend ends of electrical conduit or gas pipe. Dip in water and drag along joint to produce a smooth rounded groove.

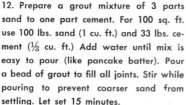

14. Remove excess grout. Grey-white grout makes an attractive contrast with Kraftile's rich brick red color—color that goes clear through, won't fade, bleach or wear off.

15. When grout has set so that it is no longer smeary, wipe off tile with clean, dry burlap.

16. Wash all tile surfaces with clean soft rags and clear water to remove cement smears.

17. When tile is thoroughly dry, apply sealing coat of Minwax. This prevents staining, makes surface easy to clean, and ready for waxing if desired. For best penetration, Minwax should be heated slightly and applied when tile surface is warm.

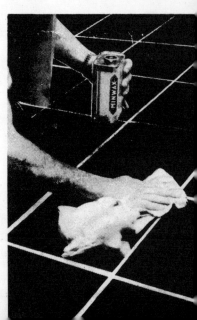

Patio—Play Areas

Whether you know it or not, if you have young children, they will think that you have built the patio for them. It is, therefore, a good idea to make some provisions for play areas when you build a patio or terrace.

If you wish to reserve the patio for adults build a play area for the children nearby. Set this play area within sight of the patio, but, if possible, do not have it adjoining the patio. A little distance between the play area and the patio can do wonders in reducing the amount of noise.

Of course, you might want a play area for grown-ups, too! There are many outdoor games which adults can play as well as children. One interesting way to solve this problem is to build a play area for the children apart from your patio and have the combination activity and game center between these two.

Factors To Consider

There are several factors which must be taken into consideration when building a play area for the children. Among these are:

1. Type of pavement—the paving material should, in general, be smooth and level. A rough paving material may look better but it's harder on young knees and harder to clean. Furthermore, the smooth surface is better for roller skating, tricycle riding and dancing.

2. Adequate drainage—once the rain stops, the youngsters will want to rush out and play, especially in the summer. It is therefore essential that the play area be paved with a material that dries quickly. Sloping the play area to enable the rain water to run off quickly is a "must" when building.

3. Sand box provisions—with young children, you must provide for a sand box. This can be a wooden box built to stand on the patio or you can leave part of the area unpaved and fill it in with sand. On the other hand, you might pave a wide border around the play area, using, for example, concrete, and leave the entire play area for sand.

4. Provisions for shade—to keep the children out of the hot sun during the afternoon in the summer, you must provide for a shaded area somewhere in the play center. Possibly a roof over a section or a small roof, made of reinforced fiberglass, supported by four posts will be sufficient to meet your requirements.

5. Have some grass—not only does grass help to break up the cold look of a paved play area but it also provides a "cushioned" surface for future football players. All youngsters like to run and tumble and a grass area within the play center is advisable. You will need a tough grass for this area. However, do not expect this grass area to look like a fine lawn. It's there to be functional and not decorative.

Checklist of Games

When planning a play area for children, consider the following games and activities and see which

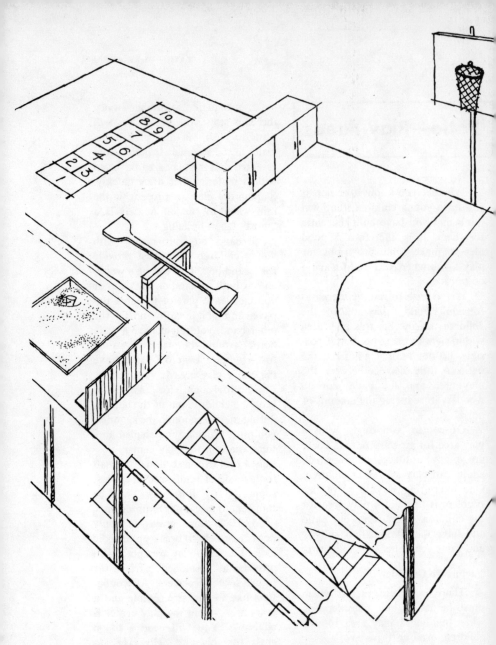

This planned play area combines features for youngsters of different ages. It requires a substantial piece of property but you can modify the design to meet your own needs and space allotment. Note that the outdoor storage cabinets with benches attached (see **Outdoor Storage**) are used to hold the various play accessories. The sand box is dug into the patio and a basketball hoop is set along the edge of the play center. For how-to details, see section on **Play Equipment for Children**. Furthermore, shade is provided by means of corrugated plastic fiberglass set on posts. For additional details on building the overhead shade unit, see discussion of roofs later in this patio section and also **Plastic Fiberglass**.

you can fit together in the space you have planned for the player center:

1. Hop-scotch—you need an area about 3'x13'— it is best to paint the lines on concrete or set divider strips in the proper place in asphalt (unless you live in hot climates).

2. Sand box—this can be made any size you wish but a 6'x6' area is a convenient size for two or three children. Don't forget your youngsters will have friends over to share in the fun.

3. Table tennis or ping pong—in order to allow for sufficient playing space, the table should be set in an area or field about 11'x17'.

4. Outdoor checkers—you can make a checker board outdoors by forming the squares out of two concrete blocks to make each square 16"x16". By using two different colors or painting alternate squares, you can make a board that is 10' 8" square. For checkers, you can use round discs, cut out of ¾" plywood or 1" stock 12" in diameter. A screw-eye in the center of each and a pole with a hook on the end to move the checkers adds to the fun.

5. Home golf—if space permits, you can build a miniature golf course. Where space is more limited, you can build a clock golf game. To do this, draw a circle about 8' to 12' in diameter and divide it into segments. In the center dig a hole about 2" to 4" in diameter and about 2" deep. The youngsters can stand in the different segments of the circle and see if they can get a hole in one.

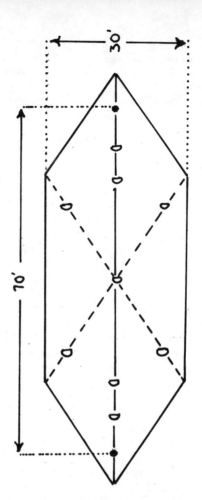

Croquet requires an area of 30'x70' but it can be laid out in a smaller space.

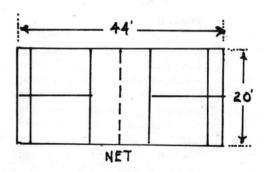

This is the lay-out plan for a badminton court; the net should be 5' high.

6. Croquet—while the official area is 36′x72′, it can be built to occupy less space. It is best to lay out this play area on short-cut grass or firmly compacted clay.

7. Badminton—the official court is 20′x44′ but with younger children you can make the court somewhat smaller. Normally, the net is 5′ high but it should be lowered for children under 12 years of age.

8. Volley ball—this requires a court 30′x60′ with a net 8′ high for adults and 6′ high for children.

9. Shuffleboard—here the children can spend many enjoyable hours and this game provides loads of fun for adults too. For each court, you need an area 6′ wide and 45′ long. If, however, you are cramped for space, a shorter court can be used, say, about 36′.

10. Horseshoes—this old game still played in many parts of the country by children and grownups alike. The over-all area is 10′ wide and 50′ long. Normally, the post centers are 40′ apart, but for the youngsters it is better to shorten this distance.

Plans for Games

If you make the play area large enough, you can set permanent areas aside for specific games. Here are several play area activities you can draw from when doing your planning. Specific dimensions are noted for each; as you will see some take a considerable amount of room and are suitable only on large patios.

For additional projects for the play area, see section on *Play Equipment for Children.*

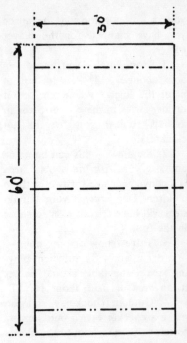

The official volley ball court is 30′x60′ but it can be made smaller for the children.

An outdoor checker board can be fun, especially when the game is played with 12″ diameter checkers with a screw-eye in the center and a pole with a hook on the end to move the checkers.

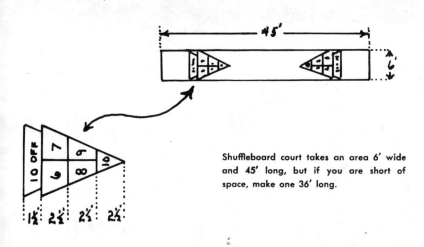

Shuffleboard court takes an area 6' wide and 45' long, but if you are short of space, make one 36' long.

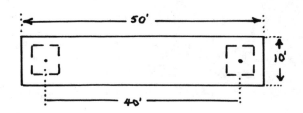

Pitching horseshoes can be fun for adults and children. Leave a 6' square area around each post and fill it with soft earth or sand.

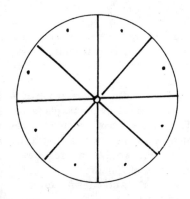

Home golf requires a circle 8' to 12' in diameter.

Plans for hop-scotch; each box is 18" deep —the big ones 36" wide and the smaller ones 18" wide.

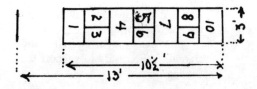

Patio—Roof

Attractive, translucent plastic fiberglass is set over a wood frame to provide a covering of the patio. Note the decorative uprights with light fixture units built into the top section, just below the roof. In the background, you can see a patio roof made of the same material as the house roof, asphalt shingles.

Photograph courtesy of Alsynite Company of America.

You can get many more hours of enjoyment out of your patio or terrace by building a roof over it. A roof over a patio built on the south side of the house provides protection from the direct rays of the hot sun. A roof over a patio built on the north side of the house enables you to use the outdoor living area despite threats of light rains from the south.

There are three factors to be considered when building a roof over your patio or terrace; they are:

1. Which material should you use for the roofing?

2. What type of uprights and framing is necessary to support the roofing?

3. Does the design blend in with your home's exterior as well as your outdoor living area?

A roof over a patio is simpler to build if the patio adjoins the house. The framing for the roof can be tied into the house's exterior wall. If the patio is away from the house, the framing for the roof is more complex.

The trend in roofing material is toward the use of plastic fiberglass. This transluscent material has many advantages for this use. It is:

• light weight and requires a minimum of framing

• easily worked with ordinary hand tools

• available in many different colors and patterns

Traditional cotton canvas is used over a metal frame to provide the necessary shade for this outdoor living area. The frame is attached to the side of the house and the outside uprights fasten to the flagstone patio. The uprights and framing can be made of Do-It-Yourself Aluminum and combined with cotton canvas.

Photograph courtesy of National Cotton Council.

• shatter-proof and fire resistant

• color-fast—no periodic finishing is required

• available in varying degrees of translucency—from practically opaque to almost transparent.

In addition to the plastic fiberglass, many other materials are used by homeowners for roofing over their out-of-doors "living room." Among the materials widely used are:

1. traditional cotton canvas—this can be set over or laced to metal or wood frames

2. standard roofing material—for example the same roofing material as on the house's roof, such as asphalt shingles

3. factory-made and assembled aluminum awnings—these are installed professionally, generally with a metal frame and metal uprights

4. basswood screens are sometimes used on a roller—this type of a roof is used only to keep the direct rays of the sun from heating the patio; the basswood screen is not effective in keeping out rain

5. colored burlap—in some parts of the country, the burlap is set in frames and inserted into a roof framing to block the sun

6. plywood—sheets of exterior-grade plywood are set over a frame and not only keep out the sun but also protect the patio from rain.

Make a Fiberglass Roof

While the framework for an exterior roof can be made of fir or pine, there are many homeowners who prefer to use redwood. This species is weather-, insect- and decay-resistant. If given a protective coat of exterior finish, the wood will remain a deep, mellow red. Without a protective coat, along the east coast, redwood loses its color and turns gray. It takes on a weatherbeaten look that is liked by many homeowners because it looks attractive and needs no maintenance.

Since building code requirements vary in different parts of the country, it's a good idea to check with the local authorities before starting your patio roof. Some towns require a building permit, while others allow you to put up a permanent roof without a permit.

For this particular patio roof, covering an area 10'x16', the rafters were made of 4x4's and set on 32" centers. The posts were also made of 4x4's but the girders were made of 4x6's.

The rafters were set on 32" centers because you can use plastic fiberglass over rafters set from 24" to 32" apart, whereas with standard roofing material, 16" center-to-center is required. The 34" Alsynite plastic fiberglass panels fit over the rafters and have an extra 2" for overlapping so that it is possible to obtain water-tight seams between panels.

Here is all the cutting you have to do:

1. Cut 2 pieces of 4x6 to the desired length of the patio roof.

2. Notch out with a saw, chisel and mallet, for the 4x4 rafters. These are placed 32" center-to-center.

3. Cut the required number of rafters to the desired depth of the patio, remembering to deduct about 3" to allow for the thickness of the two 4x6's cut in step 1.

4. Cut the cross pieces out of

1. An ordinary handsaw can be used to cut all the lumber as well as the plastic fiberglass panels needed for building the roof for this patio.

2. The cut plastic fiberglass panels are exceedingly light so that the lady of the house can help her husband with this project. Note that panel is translucent.

The individual plastic fiberglass panels are nailed to the 4x4 rafters with special nails with waterproof washers. See **Nails** and **Plastic Fiberglass**.

4x4 stock. These should be no more than 4' apart. Try to space them evenly between the wall side of the patio and the garden side.

5. The rafters and cross pieces are lap cut where they intersect. See section on *Lap Joint*.

6. Cut another piece of 4x4 the length of the 4x6's cut in step one.

7. Cut the uprights out of 4x4 and the diagonal braces too.

Putting the parts together is comparatively simple; just follow this sequence:

1. Fasten one of the 4x6's to the house wall. See *Anchors for Concrete* and *Anchors for Walls*.

2. The egg-crate is made by the lap jointing of the rafters and the cross pieces. Secure each joint with waterproof glue and several 16d

Here is another plastic fiberglass roof used over a patio. This roof has no upright supports since it is built between the garage and the house. The end pieces, attached to the house and garage, are made out of 2x8 stock while the rafters and cross pieces of the roof itself are made out of 2x6's.

This striking patio roof is fastened on three sides—one to the garage, the other to the wall over the picture window and the third to the wing of the house that extends on the right hand side of the photograph. Plastic panel roofs should be pitched 1" to the foot; this one is pitched away from the house.

aluminum nails or matching screws.

3. Nail and glue the uprights to the 4x4 cut in step 6.

4. Set the egg-crate into place so that the rafters fit into the notches provided on the 4x6 attached to the wall. Nail in place while the uprights at the forward end are supported by several boards nailed to them and held in the ground. The support boards are removed when the diagonal braces are added to the uprights.

5 Attach the diagonal bracing to the uprights; these are cut out of 4x4 stock and mitered to fit.

6. Fasten the second 4x6 to the front end of the frame.

7. Add the plastic fiberglass roof. See section on *Plastic Fiberglass*.

8. Add flashing over roof where it joins the house, and calk. Also calk the joints between the panels.

Metal uprights can be used instead of wood, if you like. These metal pillars come ready-made and are available from several manufacturers throughout the country and are often sold in lumber yards. Note the stagger effect used with the cross members between the rafters. This makes joining and nailing a simple task.

Photographs courtesy of Filon Company.

Plastic Roofing Rules

When making a patio roof out of plastic fiberglass, you will undoubtedly encounter several problems, all of which are easily solved if you have the know-how. These plastic panels generally come corrugated and it is difficult to get a perfect waterproof seal where the end of the panel butts against the flat wall.

For a weather-tight seal, you can attach the end of the corrugated panel to wood, insert small pieces of half-round and calk the openings. However, there are available matching rubber and asphalt moldings. These moldings are nailed to the wood, and the plastic panel set over the molding. It is best to use a mastic sealer between the molding and the plastic.

Where two panels join, an overlap of corrugation is necessary. The panels come with one end of the corrugations up and the other down, both sides up or both sides down. Depending upon which you get, you have to overlap from 1 to 2 corrugations to produce a weather-tight joint. You will find detailed overlapping information with the instruction sheets issued by the company whose material you purchase. Remember, use the special mastic made by these plastic companies. Although regular calking compound can be used, this special mastic is translucent and won't stick out like a sore thumb after the job is completed. This is particularly true if you use white plastic panels.

Canvas Roof with Metal Frame

Always popular is a canvas roof for a patio. In bright solid colors or stripes, the awning roof adds a decorative touch to the outdoor living area.

This metal framework is simple to construct. The canvas awning can be purchased made-to-order or it can be sewn at home. It is laced to the metal frame. Here's the how-to:

1. The pipe uprights, 1″ to 1½″ in diameter, are secured to the patio floor by means of flanges which are set into the concrete with lag screws and expansion bolts. See *Anchors for Concrete.*

2. The frame for each awning is made individually. It consists of a horizontal length of pipe with an elbow at each corner and a piece of pipe extending from the elbow to the house wall. The two ends are secured to the house by means of flanges.

3. The frames are fastened to the uprights by special ring slides, which fasten to the upright and sides of the frame.

4. The awning is equipped with grommets spaced about 6″ to 9″ apart. Each awning is laced to its frame with plastic clothesline or rope. You can remove the awning for the winter or anytime it needs repair.

5. The uprights also unscrew from the flanges on the patio floor for storage in the winter. If you use a recessed flange, you will have a perfectly smooth patio floor when the uprights are taken away for the winter.

Garden Side-Wall Shelter

Far too often a chilly fall wind or a scorching summer sun takes all the fun out of an evening outdoors. And an outdoor living area where the weather has to be just right at just the right time doesn't get too much use.

You can, however, by adding a roof, help control the climate of your outdoor living area. Many homes have their patios adjoining a door from the house. Some have picture windows or glass doors opening onto the patio. Here is a plywood shelter roof to make the outdoor living area next to your home more comfortable.

The roof of the shelter is supported on four 6x6 posts joined together with four 2x10 beams rabbeted into the top of the posts.

The posts are 14′ apart in front and back and 10′ apart along the sides, allowing for a 2′ overhang in the roof in front and a 1′ overhang at each of the sides.

At the back, a 2x4 cleat is nailed into the rear posts and the upper frame of the French doors. The cleat in back and the beam in front serve as the support for nine 2x4 rafters which are set 24″ center-to-center.

The roof over this patio was planned and built so that standard exterior fir plywood panels could be used without any cutting. The roof is just 16′ across and 12′ deep. In this way, standard 4′x8′ plywood panels—six in all—could be laid over the roof. Two panels, end-to-end, form the 16′ span. For a roof of this size, ⅜″ plywood panels were used. In areas where there is a heavy snow load and high winds, ½″ or ⅝″ plywood panels would be necessary.

This rustic garden shelter is built of framing members and six panels of exterior grade fir plywood. The roof is covered with roofing paper over the plywood panels and asphalt on top of the roofing paper. There are many other possible variations in final roof covering.

Photographs courtesy of Douglas Fir Plywood Association.

After the plywood panels are nailed in place over the rafters and beams, they should be covered with heavy roofing paper. This paper can be nailed on to the panels with special large-head roofing nails, making certain not to go through the fir plywood panels. A coat of asphalt was mopped on over the roofing paper.

The rafters and roof panels were finished before going into place. The framing is red and the underside of the roof panels were finished with white tinted with gray. In this way the plywood grain

contrast was subdued but the natural good looks of the plywood were retained.

Roof Variations

Possibly you don't like the appearance of an asphalt roof, partic-

Posts for this roof are made of 6x6 stock and are held by two double 2x10 beams. The rafters are 2x4's set 24" on center. A 1x4 is used along the perimeter of the roof to produce a finished effect.

ularly if it doesn't match your home. There are many other things that can be done with the roof.

You might leave the plywood as it is, nailed to the beams and rafters and add ½"x1" molding strips spaced 2" or 4", center-to-center. You can use astragal molding or even half-rounds to achieve an unusual effect.

Another variation you might like is covering the roof with asphalt and then sprinkling finely-crushed stone or rock over the surface so that it is embedded in the asphalt.

Where light-weight shingles are available to match your roof shingles, you can follow the technique of adding the roofing paper and then applying the shingles over the roofing paper.

If your home's roof is made of Spanish tile, you could add corrugated asbestos panels over the plywood (using the thin panels) or asbestos panels directly over the framing (if you use the thick panels). Then paint this red to match the roof tiles. The two will blend together.

A cool and comfortable roof is one that is well insulated. This is particularly true of "solid" roofs which block out all the light. An unusual roof treatment can be achieved by nailing a chicken wire mesh over the roofing paper attached to the roof. The mesh should be about ⅛" to ¼" above the roofing paper. You can use washers to accomplish this. Then prepare a mix of 1 part Portland cement, 2 parts fine, white sand and 4 parts finely crushed vermiculite. The latter is light in weight and is used in place of gravel or crushed stone in making certain types of concrete. Trowel on a ⅜" to ½" layer of this vermiculite compound over the wire mesh. It will be almost white when it dries, but you can paint it white, for white reflects the sun's rays and keeps the living space below the roof cooler and more comfortable.

Patio—Shields and Shelters

Sun shields to block the setting sun and shelters to provide many indoor comforts aid materially in family fun. How elaborate you make the sun shields or the shelters depends upon your how-to ability and your outdoor living needs.

The shields not only block out the sun but also provide privacy, especially if your patio is so situated as to have one side exposed to the street or to a neighbor's property. There are many types of shields to choose from. You can make any of those shown here or build your own based on other plans found in the section on *Fences*.

Texture One-Eleven, a special type of exterior plywood, can be used to make a very striking shield for your outdoor living area. The plywood panels are nailed to 2x4 horizontal cross members set between 4x4 uprights; see section on **Fences** for the how-to. The inserted shelves with flower pots help to break up the wall by adding focal interest spots. This shield is used to set off the play area for children from the play area for adults. When constructing it, it is best to add a 1x4 across the top and then use 1x2's to form a cap. In this way, the end grain of the plywood is protected from the elements since rain cannot penetrate into the panels.

Plastic Fiberglass can also be used to make unusual shields for the patio. Here, an extensive shield was needed since the patio is built in front of the house and the shield blocks the view from the street. While privacy was desired, the building of a solid shield or fence would have blocked out the welcome breeze. Therefore, a louver effect was used. The individual plastic panels are fastened to aluminum tubing or pipe with nuts and bolts. The tubing or pipe is set into holes in the wood cross pieces of the shield. The individual units pivot on these pipes and when closed, the panels overlap. Tilting them at an angle, blocks the unwelcome view but invites the breeze.

Umbrella Sun Shield can be made by the handyman out of pipe and cotton canvas. The upright is made in two sections with a swivel joint between them. The lower section is fastened in the ground, either to a flange or set in concrete. The frame is made of four pieces of pipe with four elbows. The diagonal braces, also made of pipe, are welded to the frame and connected to the upper section of the upright. The canvas cover is laced to the pipe frame. If you wish, you can make the top frame out of wood poles, 1" or larger in diameter, but pipe is stronger and will stand up better in the wind and rain.

Photograph courtesy of the National Cotton Council.

The Barbecue Port

For the last word in outdoor living, you can build this barbecue port or modify it to meet your individual requirements. This plan calls for an extension of the carport into a breezy, cheery summer dining room. The locker addition to the outside of the carport, if you don't have one there now, provides extra storage space. See sections on *Outdoor Storage* and *Carport* for additional storage space ideas.

The angled plastic fiberglass panels provide coolness and privacy in a colorful "extra room" for recreation, dining and entertaining. The plastic roof provides the necessary shade and permits you to use this "extra room" in almost any weather during the late spring, summer and early fall. Note that a decorative touch is added by making the planter walls on the outside of the patio out of plastic.

To make this handsome addition, start by laying the patio floor. You can use any material that blends in with your home. Although

the carport is made of concrete, the floor of the patio is made of colorful flagstone and one section of brick. To provide for comfort on a cool evening as well as a place to cook meals outdoors, add a barbecue. See section on *Barbecues*.

The framing for the roof follows the same procedure as outlined earlier in the section on patio roofs as well as the detailed plans on the following pages. With the framework complete, the plastic panels can be set in place. For full how-to with plastic fiberglass panels, see the section on *Plastic Fiberglass*.

Materials Needed

3x6's for long studs along the two sides of the patio

2x12's for the louver sill and plate

2x6's for the top plates of the patio roof

4x4's for the room beam, where the plastic fiberglass roof framing is joined to the exterior wall.

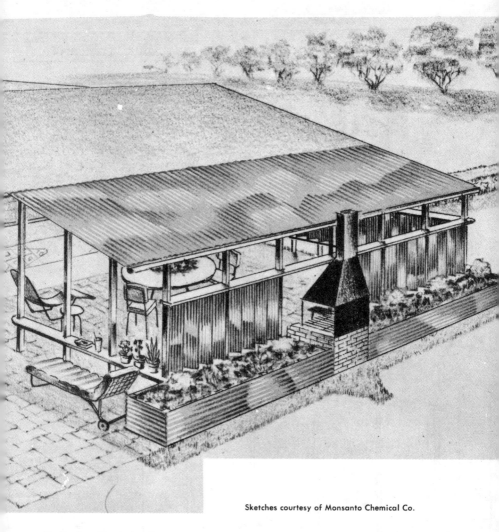

Sketches courtesy of Monsanto Chemical Co.

2x4's for the end rafters

2x4's for the purlins

2x6's for the roof rafters

1x6's for the facia board

1x3's for the contour strips for the vertical louvers

3x3's of cypress for the planter posts

6d, 8d and 10d common and finishing nails used for framing

Brass screws for fastening the contour strips

Roofing nails with neoprene washers for nailing the plastic fiberglass panels to the wood framing

Closure strips between the panels and top of all purlins; see manufacturer's details and recommendations with the panels

Corrugated plastic fiberglass panels, allowing for 1 full lap on the sides when the panels are joined

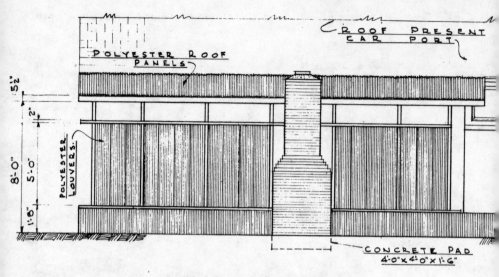

Detailed view of side—louver plastic panels are 5' high and fit above the 20" planter. The barbecue can be made according to your own plans; see **Barbecue** section for additional plans.

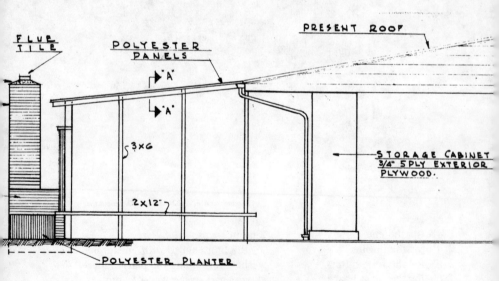

Front view of the barbecue port—3x6's are used as studs, 2x6's as plates and 2x4's as rafters. For detailed cross-section of stud-plate-rafter, see illustration.

This is a view looking down on the barbecue port. While it shows how you can add this deluxe outdoor "room" to your carport, it can be modified to your specific needs. It can be added to the exterior wall of any home.

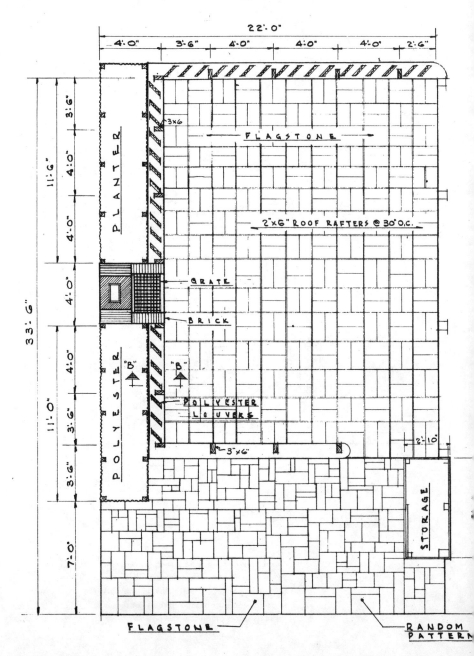

Detailed view of stud-plate-rafter joint—
cross-section view as noted on the front
elevation sketch.

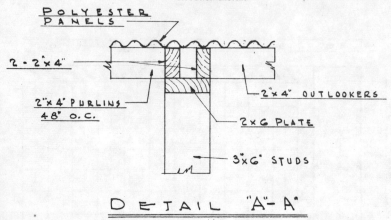

POLYESTER
PANELS

2 - 2"x 4"

2"x 4" PURLINS
48" O.C.

2"x 4" OUTLOOKERS

2 x 6 PLATE

3"x 6" STUDS

DETAIL "A-A"

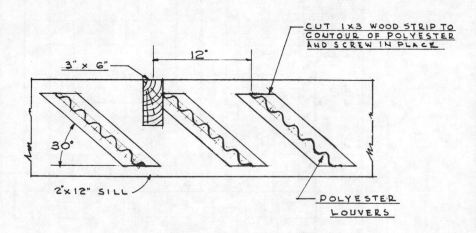

CUT 1x3 WOOD STRIP TO
CONTOUR OF POLYESTER
AND SCREW IN PLACE

3" x 6"

12"

30°

2"x 12" SILL

POLYESTER
LOUVERS

DETAIL "B-B"

This is how the plastic panel louvers are
set in place along the outside wall of the
barbecue port. Cut 1x3 strips to the corrugated contour of the panels and use
these as cleats along top and bottom.

Cabana Room

This "Cabana Room," developed by a San Jose, California, builder, actually is a sheltered, shaded outdoor living area with barbecue facilities, a fir plywood-decked roof on simple posts and beams, plus a handy outdoor storage unit. While the photographs here show several different views, you will find that there are individual projects which you can incorporate into your patio plans.

The actual area required for this specific unit is 15'x30'. The house, garage and property-line fence form three sides of the area and the fourth opens onto the garden.

The patio floor of poured concrete is decorated by setting a few 2x4 pieces or redwood into it. This helps to break up the cold look of the concrete.

The roof rests of 4x4 posts and beams with 2x4's used as rafters The roof itself is made of ⅜" exterior fir plywood which is nailed directly to the 2x4 rafters. Instead of adding roofing paper and asphalt, plastic glass was used to cover this roof. It produces a tough long-lasting finish on the plywood and its shiny surface helps to bounce off the sun's rays.

Among some of the highlights of this outdoor living area are a large outdoor storage closet, conveniently located at the back of the shelter right next to the garden, an attractive pool in one corner, a storage chest-seat combination and ample room for entertaining, dining and dancing.

To take away the cold feeling of plain wood and concrete, planter boxes were utilized on this patio. A planter box made of brick adds a decorative touch around the pool. Individual planter units, made out of lumber, were spotted here and there on the concrete floor. The use of planters can do wonders for most patios. Although they are outdoors and are designed to blend in with the garden, too many patios—especially those adjoining the house—are "cold" areas. A planter built into the ground or a planter box set on the patio floor near the house adds color and warmth. See section on *Planters*.

Large storage cabinet forms part of one side of this patio unit. The doors and sides can be made of tongue-and-groove boards, but the handyman will find it easier to make the unit out of plywood panels.

The house forms another side of this outdoor living area. Note the storage chestseat units. The chests are built 15" high and 15" deep and as long as you need. The top is hinged to the back and is easy to lift whenever you need anything from the inside.

The lily pool with a brick planter is the focal spot of this out-of-doors "extra room." Because of the mild climate, an aviary was added to brighten this corner. Note that a section of the roof is left open so that the sun can shine in on the plants.

Peeling

This is an advanced stage of a paint failure. It differs from alligatoring in that the cracks extend through the surface coatings all the way down to the wood surface. When this condition occurs, it is essential that the entire painted surface be removed either by sanding or with a paint remover.

Peeling is caused either by:
- poor elasticity of the paint because of insufficient oil or,
- improper brushing of the paint, leaving too heavy an accumulation of oil or pigments on the surface.

An advanced stage of peeling.

Photograph courtesy of Wilson Imperial Co.

- -

Peg-Board

Although commonly used to describe perforated hardboard, "Peg-Board" is a registered trademark. See *Perforated Hardboard*.

- -

Peining

The beating over or smoothing over a metallic surface, such as a rivet, with the pein end of a ball pein hammer. See *Ball Pein Hammer*.

- -

Perforated Hardboard

Perforated hardboard comes in many different sizes and thicknesses and has many uses within the home. It is available:
- in small pieces about 2′ square to full size 4′x8′ panels
- in panels and pieces ⅛″ thick with 3/16″ diameter holes
- in panels and pieces ¼″ thick with 9/32″ diameter holes.

Perforated hardboard is used here as a decorative accent! It also provides hanging room for book shelves, magazine rack and end table.

• with holes spaced ½″ or 1″ on center.

While most perforated hardboard comes in the standard brown color of standard hardboard, some panels are available in color and others with a textured surface. Furthermore, perforated hardboard is also available in corrugated panels.

Hangers and Hooks

There are a great number of special hangers and hooks which fit into the holes in the perforated board. This makes it possible to hang things on the panels for decorative effects or for storage.

By using these hooks and hangers, it is possible to put to work the walls inside the closet, workshop, garage, kitchen; in fact, any room of the house. The accompanying

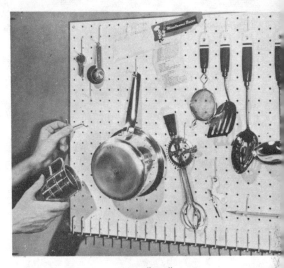

Handy in the kitchen, this 20″x23″ Peg-Board comes with hooks and clips and can be attached, with washers, to the wall or a door.

Photographs courtesy of Masonite Corp.

Convenient for children, the perforated hardboard unit is attached to the inside of the closet door. It helps the youngsters keep closets neat and provides a handy place to keep small items which can be misplaced easily.

A larger panel in the garage, holds hand tools as well as garden tools—everything needed for outside maintenance.

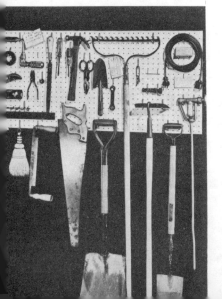

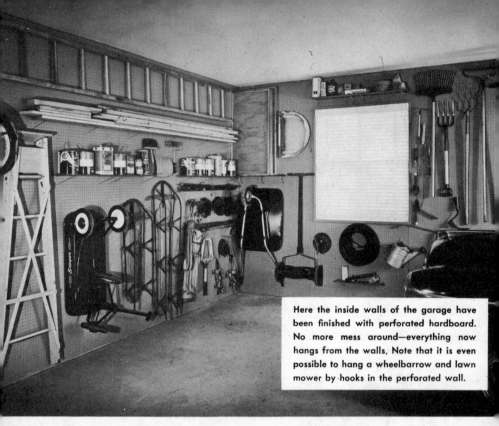

Here the inside walls of the garage have been finished with perforated hardboard. No more mess around—everything now hangs from the walls. Note that it is even possible to hang a wheelbarrow and lawn mower by hooks in the perforated wall.

If you're an outdoor enthusiast, you will find a perforated hardboard wall in the basement a handy place to store all your equipment. The many different hook and hanger attachments make it possible to set everything on the wall, even an outboard motor.

photographs show some of the uses to which perforated hardboard can be put.

Attaching Perforated Board

Several different methods can be used to install perforated hardboard within the home.

1. Perforated hardboard can be applied directly over studs in the same manner as standard or tempered hardboard. It can be nailed or screwed directly to the wood. See *Hardboard*.

2. It can be placed on existing

walls. However, to take advantage of the perforations for hooks and hangers, the panel must be kept about ¼″ away from the existing wall. This can be done either by placing washers between the panel and the wall and setting screws through the panel and washer into the existing wall, or the perforated hardboard can be set on ¼″ thick furring strips set about 24″ apart, horizontally across the wall.

3. Perforated hardboard can also be set directly over masonry walls. Special metal hangers with built-in washers can be glued to the concrete, brick or stone with a special adhesive. The panels are attached to these hangers by means of threaded bolts.

4. These panels can be used in partition walls as single wall units. The hardboard panels can be set within a frame and then placed between the plates and studs of the wall. See *Wall Framing*.

If wall space is available in the pantry, you can use perforated hardboard effectively for storing cleaning aids.

Here's how this perforated panel material can be used in a young child's room. The upper section of the wall can be used to store items used outdoors. The items along the lower part of the wall are easily reached by the youngster.

Photographs courtesy of Masonite Corp.

Anchor kits are available for attaching perforated hardboard to concrete, brick or any smooth wall surface. Each kit contains 10 anchors and 10 bolts plus a can of adhesive. The kit is sufficient to attach a 4′x4′ panel, and no special tools are required. All you need is a putty knife to spread the adhesive and screwdriver to tighten the bolts.

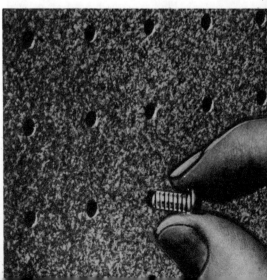

Pergola

This is an arbor or trellis with sides and a top over which vines will grow and climb. See *Arbor* and *Trellis*.

Perimeter

The outer boundary of any plane surface is its perimeter. To determine the perimeter of a patio 20'x 30', you add the four sides—20, 30, 20 and 30 or a total of 100'. The perimeter of a circle is called its circumference.

Perpendicular

The joining of a line or a surface at right angles or 90° is termed perpendicular. If the angle between the two lines or surfaces is greater than 90°, then an obtuse angle is formed. If the angle is less than a right angle or 90°, it is called an acute angle.

Phillips Screw

Available in a variety of head forms, such as flat, round, pan, etc., a Phillips screw has a four-pointed star-shaped recess in the head. It requires a special screwdriver for setting. Phillips screws are used frequently in automobile body work and for holding metal parts of appliances together.
See *Screws*.

Top view of a Phillips head screw.

Phillips Screwdriver

A specially shaped screwdriver designed for use with Phillips

Phillips screwdrivers come in different sizes to fit the various Phillips screws.

screws, it has an almost pointed end with four fins or wedges that fit into the screw. There is less chance of slipping with a screwdriver when using a Phillips screw. and screwdriver.

See *Screwdrivers* for additional details.

Phonograph Slide

Special hardware is used in most factory-made radio-phonographs to enable the user to pull the phonograph out of the cabinet in order to change the records. While this special hardware, called phonograph slides, served originally for this purpose, it has become widely used in other furniture and cabinets.

The slide consists of two metal pieces with rollers or ball bearings. One part is attached to the side of the drawer or shelf and the other part to the inside face of the cabinet. Slides are sometimes mounted on the bottom of the drawer as well. But, in either case, slides are used in pairs.

Phonograph slides are made in various lengths and styles depending upon the load they will support. Some are available in many hardware stores, but only the specialty dealers carry a fairly complete line of slides.

One modification in phonograph slides is the use of pre-formed metal channels in which shelves can ride. These are exceedingly popular in kitchen units as well as radio-phonograph units. A metal channel is fastened to the inside face of the cabinet sides and the drawer base or shelf rides in the channel.

Shelf guides, a modification of phonograph slides, are used in this kitchen cabinet to make it easy to reach the storage shelves inside without putting your hand all the way in. The shelf slides out so that everything on it is easily accessible.

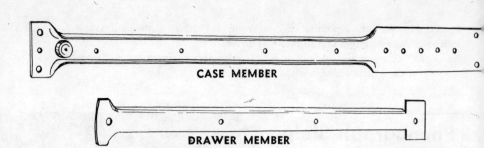

CASE MEMBER

DRAWER MEMBER

Shelf guides are made to accommodate shelves up to ¾" thick. The guides can be used with drawers if each side is set in ½" from the side edge of the bottom of the drawer. See **Built-Ins** for examples of this technique in use.

Photograph and sketches courtesy of Washington Steel Products, Inc.

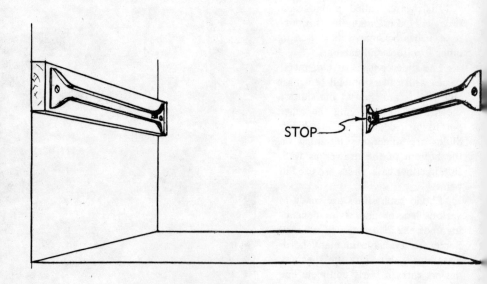

STOP

Two major parts of a drawer guide or a light-weight phonograph slide. The case member is attached to the inside face of the cabinet side; the long flat end can be bent depending upon the depth of the cabinet. The drawer member is attached to the side of the drawer.

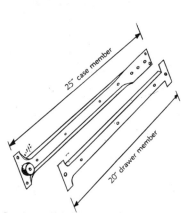

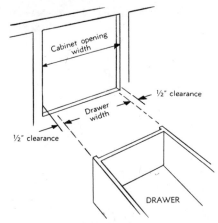

1. This model drawer guide is adjustable to fit various depth drawers and can be used on either the right-hand or left-hand side of the drawer. The heavy-duty models are generally made with one slide for the right side and other for the left.

2. It is necessary to provide a ½" clearance on either side of the drawer to allow for the thickness of the drawer guide. When making your own cabinets or furniture, make the frame first and then the drawer to the required size.

How To Install a Drawer Guide

3. Unpack the guides when you bring them home and are ready to install them in the cabinet. Lay them down as shown so that you have two pairs—a case member and a drawer member for each side of the drawer you plan to install.

4. Set the front end of the case member into the corner of the cabinet opening and attach it with two screws. Measure its exact position and then set the other case member into place on the other side of the cabinet.

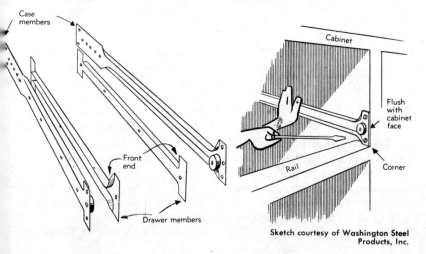

Sketch courtesy of Washington Steel Products, Inc.

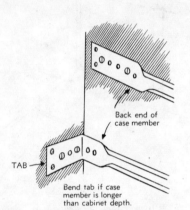

Back end of case member

TAB

Bend tab if case member is longer than cabinet depth.

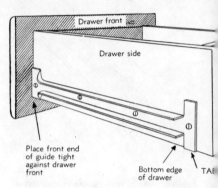

Drawer front

Drawer side

Place front end of guide tight against drawer front

Bottom edge of drawer

TAB

5. If the case member is shorter than the cabinet depth, you can fasten the back end of the unit with a single screw through the last hole and another screw through one of the other holes. If it is longer, just bend the case member and screw into place.

6. The drawer member of the slide is fastened so that it is flush with the front edge, just behind the rabbetted face and level with the bottom edge of the drawer. Use the four screws to fasten the unit to the drawer side; then attach the other side and slip drawer into place.

Photo Mural Walls

Photographic blow-ups of your favorite picture or ready-made enlargements are available and can be mounted in the same manner as wallpaper. For complete how-to see *Mural Walls* and *Wallpapering*.

Piano Care

Temperature plays an important part in the piano's well-being; therefore, it must not be placed in any spot where there is heat from a radiator, or cold air from an open window, or where there is any dampness in the atmosphere.

If the house is to be closed during the winter, and no warmth supplied, protect the piano by wrapping and tying around it several thicknesses of heavy paper or cloth. This will prevent dampness and cold from harming the instrument.

If moths are a problem in your house, place a piece of gum camphor inside the piano as a protection for the felt hammers which may attract moths.

Piano keys may be cleaned by

rubbing with a soft cloth dipped in rubbing alcohol, then wiping off with a dry cloth.

If the keys are covered all the time they may turn yellow; it is a good idea to keep the lid open as much as possible so the piano keys will receive the light they need.

Piano Hinge

A piano hinge resembles a butt hinge in construction but comes in continuous lengths up to 8′ and longer. It is used to hinge parts together where there will be excessive stress on the hinge, such as a table leaf. See *Hinges*.

A piano hinge used to hold a table leaf.

Pick-Up Tongs, Extension

These tongs may not be used very often; but when you need them, they are worth their weight in gold. With extension tongs you can reach into tight places, even around corners and into holes, to recover dropped bolts, nuts, screws, keys, pins and the like.

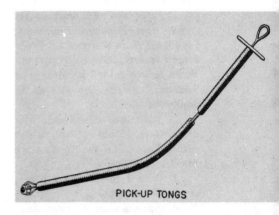

PICK-UP TONGS

Pickled Finish

The pickled finish produces very pleasing results when refinishing old furniture or finishing new work. The best results are obtained when working on open-grained woods, like oak and chestnut.

Equipment you need: To produce a pickled finish, you should have:

• a bleaching agent to lighten

the wood. You can purchase a number of bleaches in any paint supply or hardware store. Many come in bottles marked #1 and #2.

- rubber gloves
- goggles
- rubber apron or old clothes
- cotton dish mop to apply the bleach
- a scrubbing brush for washing
- thick white paint or a paste made of equal parts of turpentine and boiled linseed oil combined with white lead
- cloths for wiping
- grade 0 steel wool
- sandpaper
- varnish or any other suitable finishing material

To produce a pickled finish follow this procedure:

1. After the old finish is removed (see *Furniture Finishing*), bleach the piece of wood. Apply the bleach as directed on the bottles until the desired color is obtained. For additional details, see section on *Bleaching*.

2. Wash the surface clean with clear water, scrubbing with a stiff brush. Then allow the wood to dry for at least 48 hours.

3. With a fine abrasive paper, smooth the surface.

4. Apply a sealer coat and when dry, smooth with fine 0 grade steel wool and brush clean.

5. Apply either white paint or the white lead mixture with a cloth, rubbing its crosswise into the grain. Spread this on evenly, wiping off all the excess not required to fill the grain, but leaving a thin film over the surface.

6. After the white paint or the

Applying the varnish coat to a piece of pickled oak.

white lead mixture has dried, rub the surface against the grain with 0 grade steel wool until all the white has been removed from the surface. Do not rub the white paint or lead out of the grain.

7. Apply varnish or any other suitable finish.

For further details, see *Furniture Finishing*.

Picture Molding

See *Framing a Picture* and *Moldings.*

Pigment

A pigment is a white or colored substance which comes in powder or paste form and which is added to paint to give it:

- body
- opacity or covering power
- and color.

However, few pigments can produce all three effects in paints and, therefore, several pigments are often used in paint to produce the desired effect.

Typical Pigments

Certain basic pigments are used in many paints and an understanding of their qualities will help you in the selection of paint. Among the more commonly used pigments are:

1. White lead—it is probably the most opaque and durable of all white pigments and is excellent for exterior painting. However, it chalks or powders off the surface after a few years. This can be avoided by adding colored pigments or by the addition of about 15% to 20% of zinc oxide. Along the coast, where salt air causes white lead to chalk more quickly, a higher percentage of zinc oxide is needed.

2. Zinc oxide—it is mostly used to produce enamel paints but it is also used to "toughen" white lead paints.

3. Titanium—this pigment retains its white color well and will stand up in industrial areas where there are many gases and impurities in the air. It has great hiding or covering power and is often combined with 15% to 20% of zinc oxide.

4. Lithopane—this is a trade name given to the mixture of two chemicals, zinc sulphide and barium sulphate. It is used widely in flat white paints because of its great covering power. It is non-poisonous and used frequently for painting children's rooms and toys.

5. Red lead—this brilliant red pigment is used as the base for many of the metal paints.

6. Blue lead—it has greater spreading power than red lead and is also a good rust inhibitor. Furthermore, it provides a better base for the final coat of paint than red lead.

7. Whiting—a form of calcium carbonate, it is used mainly for making calcimine water paint and also is combined with white lead and linseed oil to make putty.

Pigtail

A pigtail splice, or pigtail, as it is commonly called, is a splice or joining of two wires by twisting together the bared ends of parallel conductors.

Pilot Hole

This term is used to describe a hole drilled, primarily in hardwood, to guide a screw or sometimes a nail into position.

Pilot Light, Gas

For a description of how the pilot light operates, refer to the section on *Gas Appliances,* and specifically to the part in that section which discusses "*Operation and Care.*"

Pincers

Similar to a pliers, a pincers has a pair of grasping jaws for handling or holding an object. Pincers are also used for cutting off protruding nails from a board.

Photograph courtesy of Diamond Calk
Horseshoe Co.

Pinch Bar

This is another name for a crow-bar.

Ping-Pong Table

For complete plans to make a fold-away ping-pong table see *Furniture*.

Easy-to-make ping-pong table of fir plywood.

Pins, Taper

See *Keys and Pins*.

Pipe Cutter

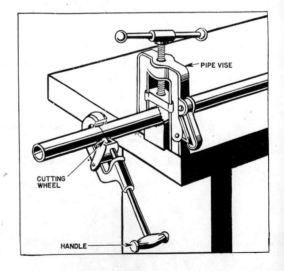

Copper pipe and tubing as well as other thin-wall pipe can be cut with either hacksaw or a pipe cutter. Pipe cutters come in various sizes, but the homeowner has little use for the larger models. A cutter capable of cutting pipe or tubing up to 1″ in diameter is sufficient for general home use.

A pipe cutter is used for cutting copper pipe and tubing and other thin-wall pipe.

.The cutter rotates around the pipe or tubing and the cutting wheel "eats" its way through the pipe wall. As the cutter is revolved, the handle is tightened periodically and this causes the cutting wheel to go deeper into the pipe wall.

Always make certain that the pipe or tubing is securely held when cutting. Turn the handle ¼ to ½ turn at a time and then revolve one full turn; repeat the tightening and turning until the pipe or tubing is cut.

Pipe Fittings

Pipe fittings are used to join pipes to each other, to connect pipe to fixtures and to change the direction of the pipe. Pipes up to 2″ in diameter are usually joined by fittings. For additional details and how-to data, see *Plumbing*.

There are many different types of pipe fittings designed to do practically every type of connection. Here are a few of the many different fittings for iron and brass pipe plus their use:

1. Close nipple—used to connect two pipes with female threads (that is, threaded on the inside) or to connect a pipe and a plumbing fixture with female threads.

2. Straight T with reducer leg—used to join thread pipes with male threads (that is, threaded on the outside); two pipes have the same diameter and the third is one size smaller.

3. Reducer—used to join two pipes with male threads of different diameters.

4. Plug—used to close an end of pipe with a female thread.

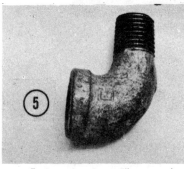

5. Street L or Street Elbow—used to join two pipes at a right angle, with one pipe having a male thread and the other a female thread.

6. Union—used to join two pipes with male threads; the union can be opened at any time without disturbing the rest of the plumbing.

7. Elbow or 90° L—used to join two pipes of the same diameter with male threads at a right angle.

8. Hose adaptor—used at the end of a male threaded pipe for attaching a hose; the male end of the adaptor has garden hose thread for connecting washing machine hoses, dishwasher hose or garden hose.

9. Straight T—used to join three pipes of the same diameter with male threads; one pipe is at right angles to the other two which form a straight line.

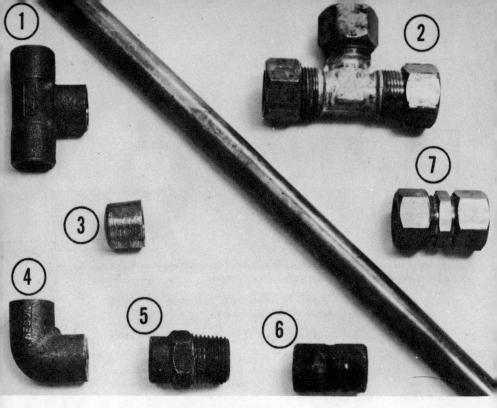

Pipe fittings for copper tubing come in two types—one type is soldered and the other flared and held by compression nuts. Here are some typical fittings of both types: (1) a solder T, (2) a solderless or compression T, (3) a cap to close an end of the pipe—the cap must be soldered on, (4) a 90° solder-type elbow, (5) an adaptor for brass or iron pipe—female end is soldered on to the copper tubing and the external thread end is inserted into iron or brass pipe, (6) a solder-type coupling to join two pieces of tubing, and (7) a solderless-type coupling to join two copper tubing pieces.

A flange is used to attach pipe to a wood or masonry surface. It is not generally used in ordinary plumbing for pipes carrying water, fuel or gas. It is used, for example, to attach pipe legs to the underside of a wooden table.

Pipe Tongs

Also known as chain tongs, a pipe tongs is a wrench that has a chain, similar to that used on a bicycle, for gripping and holding a pipe. It is used primarily with pipes over 2″ in diameter.

Pipe Vise

There are two types of pipe vises: (1) a hinged-side type with V jaws to hold small pipes and (2) the chain type which is used with large diameter pipes. See *Plumbing*.

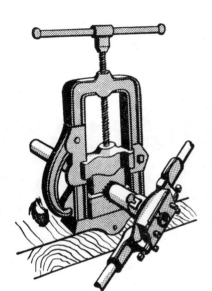

Pipe being held in a pipe vise while being threaded.

Machinist's vise can be used to hold pipe by means of special pipe jaws.

Pipe Wrench

This is an adjustable tool; it is often called a Stillson wrench. It is used for turning pipe, round rod, or smooth fittings which do not offer a gripping surface for other types of wrenches. However, the bite of the jaws often leaves marks on the work. The pipe wrench should not be used on nuts or bolts.

See the section on *Wrenches*.

Pipes, Condensation

To prevent pipes, particularly cold water pipes, from "sweating" in hot weather, special coverings are used over the pipes. See *Condensation*.

One way to prevent condensation is to wrap the pipe with a special impregnated covering.

Pipes, Frozen

For details on thawing frozen pipes, see *Frozen Pipes*.

Plain Sawing

Lumber is termed "plain sawn" when the saw cuts are taken parallel to the squared side of a log.

Planer-Jointer

See *Jointer*.

Planes

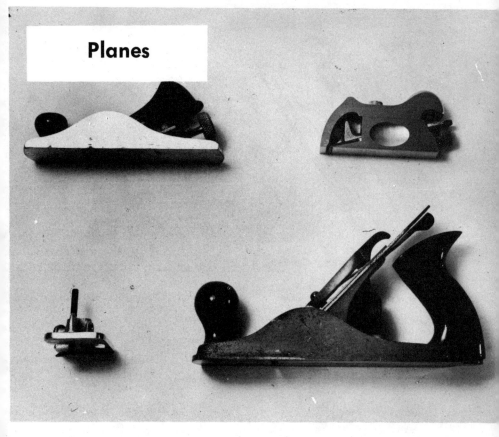

Planes for the handyman's workshop (clockwise from upper left): block plane, bullnose rabbet plane, smooth plane and router plane.

The various types of planes are discussed under their own headings. Refer to the separate sections on *Combination, Dado, Fore, Jack, Jointer, Rabbet,* and *Smooth Plane.*

Generally, the following information applies to the different types of planes.

The cutting part of the plane is referred to as the plane iron. In most general purpose planes, it is double and consists of a single plane iron and a plane iron cap, with a cap screw to hold them together. This double plane iron assembly is held tightly in the plane bed by a spring-type lever cap.

If the plane cuts too much, or not enough, adjust the depth of cut with the depth-adjustment knob, which is located in front of the handle. If the cutting edge removes more wood on one side than on the other, adjust the double plane iron

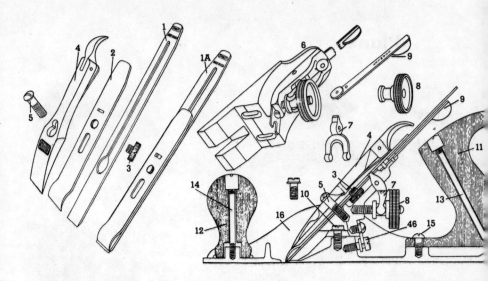

1A DOUBLE PLANE IRON	**4** LEVER CAP	**9** LATERAL ADJUSTING LEVER	**14** KNOB BOLT & NUT
1 SINGLE " "	**5** " " SCREW	**10** FROG SCREW	**15** HANDLE SCREW
2 PLANE IRON CAP	**6** FROG COMPLETE	**11** HANDLE	**16** BOTTOM
3 CAP SCREW	**7** "Y" ADJUSTING LEVER	**12** KNOB	**46** FROG ADJUSTING SCR
	8 ADJUSTING NUT	**13** HANDLE BOLT & NUT	

Sketches from "Tool Guide" courtesy o
Stanley Tool

Basic parts of a plane

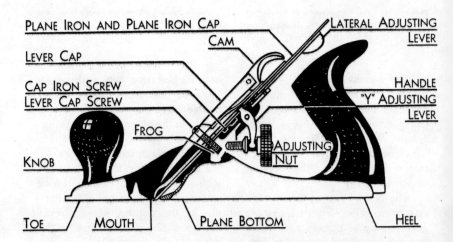

sidewise with the lateral adjusting lever.

Grinding Plane Irons

Irons must be ground when cutting edge is nicked, when bevel is worn too blunt, when bevel is rounded out, or when cutting edge is worn to improper shape.

1. Cutting edges should be straight on smooth and block plane irons, slightly curved on jack plane irons, and very slightly curved on fore plane irons.

2. Bevel may be straight or slightly concave. It must never be rounded out.

3. Bevel should be about twice the thickness of iron near cutting edge.

Caution: While grinding, keep plane bit cool by frequently dipping into water to prevent burning or softening of the steel. Keep the fingers near the grinding edge while grinding to feel and determine if plane iron is becoming too hot.

1. Square cutting edge, and remove nicks as necessary.

2. Adjust rest on grinder to a position which will give correct bevel.

3. Grind by moving iron from side to side to grind all parts of bevel evenly, and square with the edges.

Note: Special holding devices are available for sharpening plane bits. Their use simplifies the grinding.

Sharpening Plane Irons

Always sharpen iron after grinding. During use of plane, sharpen

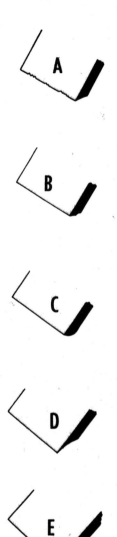

When to grind a plane iron: (a) the cutting edge is nicked, (b) the bevel has been worn down by too much whetting, (c) the bevel has been rounded by careless whetting, (d) the bevel is too long and thin; since it is weak, it will nick easily and (e) the bevel is too short and thick so that it will not enter the wood easily.

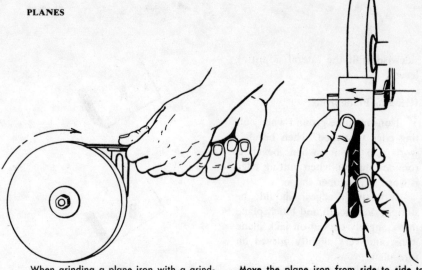

When grinding a plane iron with a grindstone, the stone should turn toward the iron. Use the guide to maintain a flat, even bevel. To keep the plane iron from burning or softening, keep the iron cool by dipping it into water frequently.

Move the plane iron from side to side to grind all parts on the bevel. The edge should be straight and at right angles to the center line of the plane iron.

Whet the plane iron on an oilstone to produce a really sharp cutting edge. Hold the plane iron so that the bevel is on the stone with the back edge slightly raised. Move the plane iron back and forth.

To remove the wire or feather edge, take a few strokes with the flat side of the plane iron held flat on the stone.

Sketches from "Tool Guide" courtesy of
Stanley Tools.

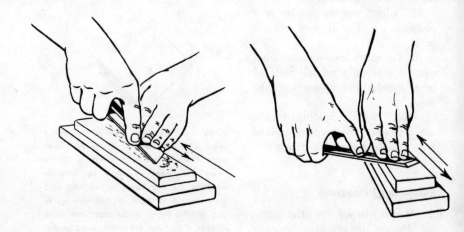

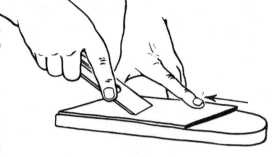

Finish whetting the plane iron with a few strokes on a leather strop to produce a keener edge.

iron as often as necessary to keep a keen edge.

1. Grasp iron with both hands, palms downward. Place iron bevel on lightly oiled stone with iron at bevel angle.

2. Apply light pressure to iron and rub back and forth over surface of stone. Do not alter angle of iron to stone during process. Round off corners enough to allow for depth of cut.

3. After whetting bevel side, turn iron over and hold perfectly flat on stone. Give it two or three strokes to remove wire edge.

Regrinding Chip Cap

The chip cap is made of soft steel and the sharp edge is easily dented or marred, thus requiring regrinding.

1. Separate the chip cap and plane iron and remove the chip cap screw.

2. Grind the lower surface of the curved end on the side of a grinding wheel.

3. Grind only as required to remove nicks.

4. Finish grinding surface, and remove wire edge on an oilstone.

Setting Iron

Jack, fore, and smooth planes have double plane irons. A chip cap is secured to iron by a set screw. This chip cap breaks the shaving as soon as possible after it is cut. Depth of cut is regulated by a depth screw. Set chip cap back farther for

a coarse chip or shaving than for a fine one. Never allow chip cap corners to extend beyond cutting edge of plane iron; it must always be back of cutting edge. A block plane, having a single plane iron, has no chip cap.

1. Test fit of chip cap on iron. It must fit without gapping to pre-

Basic parts of a double plane iron.

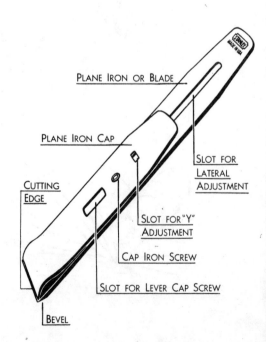

PLANE IRON OR BLADE

PLANE IRON CAP

CUTTING EDGE

SLOT FOR LATERAL ADJUSTMENT

SLOT FOR "Y" ADJUSTMENT

CAP IRON SCREW

SLOT FOR LEVER CAP SCREW

BEVEL

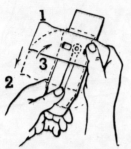

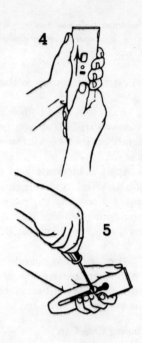

To put the plane iron and the plane iron cap together, you should: (1) lay the plane iron cap on the flat side of the plane iron, (2) draw the plane iron cap back, (3) turn it straight with the plane iron, (4) then advance the plane iron cap until the edge is just back of the cutting edge of the plane iron, and (5) finally, hold the plane iron and the plane iron cap firmly and tighten the screw to hold the two parts together.

POORLY FITTED

PROPERLY FITTED

Edges of the plane iron cap must fit tight to prevent shavings from wedging under it, piling up and choking the plane. Therefore, be careful when adjusting the plane iron cap and the plane iron.

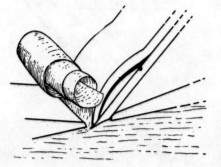

The plane iron cap breaks and curls the shaving. Together with the toe of the plane, it prevents the wood from splitting ahead of the cutting edge, thereby producing a smooth surface. The plane iron cap also serves to stiffen the plane iron.

How To Set a Plane

1. To put a plane together, lay the plane iron, bevel side down, on the frog. Be sure the roller on the lateral adjusting lever and the head of the plane iron cap screw are correctly seated.

2. Slip the lever cap under the lever cap screw and press down the cam. If the plane iron is in the correct position, the cam will snap into place easily. If the cam does not, loosen the lever cap screw slightly. If the plane iron is not firmly held when the cam is in place, tighten the lever cap screw.

3. The plane iron should be pushed out when the adjusting nut is moved out toward the handle. Conversely, the plane iron is drawn in when the adjusting nut is moved toward the frog.

4. To adjust for the evenness of the shaving, sight along the bottom of the plane and move the lateral adjusting lever toward the right or the left.

5. Here is a phantom view with the knob, lever cap and plane iron cap removed to show the action of the lateral adjusting lever.

vent shavings from forcing themselves between chip cap and iron. If not a close fit, sharpen chip cap on an oilstone. Hold chip cap so as to preserve original angle while sharpening.

2. Enter cap set screw into slot in iron. Adjust cap to ¹⁄₆₄″ from cutting edge of iron, and parallel with cutting edge. Tighten set screw.

3. Adjust "set" (distance between cutting edge of iron and edge of chip cap) by lightly tapping end of blade opposite cutting edge.

How To Use a Plane

1. To start planing, take an easy but firm position directly in back of the work.

Sketches from "Tool Guide" courtesy of Stanley Tools.

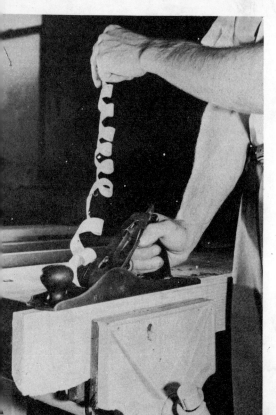

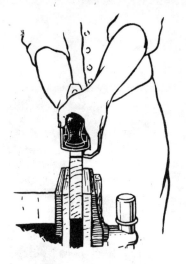

2. Hold the plane square with the work face of the work.

3. At the end of the stroke, the weight of your body should be carried easily on the left foot.

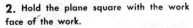

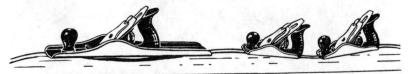

It is easier to plane a long straight edge with a long plane than with a short one. A long plane, such as a jointer plane, bridges the low parts and does not cut them until the high spots are removed.

To cut a smooth, straight edge, the plane is pushed with the grain. To keep the plane straight, press down on the knob at the beginning of the stroke and on the handle at the end of the stroke. Avoid dropping the plane (shown by the broken lines) for this will round the corners.

When planing end grain, plane half way from each edge to avoid splitting the corners.

If the plane is pushed all the way, the corners of the work will break as shown here.

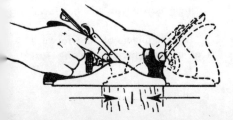

Adjusting Frog—

Frogs must be set square with plane sides and set forward with sufficient clearance for chips to pass through without clogging.

Using the Plane

Determine the general direction of the grain of the wood before you start to plane. Plane with the grain—not against it. When you've decided in which direction to cut, clamp the stock securely in the vise or on the bench top. When stock is held in the vise, protect it with pieces of scrap wood— otherwise the vise jaws will scar the surface.

Push the plane with steady, level strokes. Start the cut with extra pressure on the front of the plane bed. Push the plane the entire length of the stock, and finish the stroke with added pressure on the after part of the plane. This method prevents rounded corners.

To make planing easier when you're taking a rough cut, slant the plane across the stock as you push it forward. This method allows the cutting edge of the plane to slice off the shavings. You probably use the same principle when you shave with a safety razor by holding it at an angle as you trim off your facial foliage.

Use the fingers of your forward hand to guide the plane along. Just keep your thumb on top to exert downward pressure, and let the fingers slide under the plane to do the guiding. But before you guide with your fingers, be sure the surface of the stock is smooth! Splinters are tricky, and they don't sound off with a warning signal.

When you plane the end grain of a board you can use the jack plane or smooth plane but a block plane is better if one is available, because it is specially designed for cutting end grain. Its plane iron, or blade, is set at a very small angle with the bottom of the bed to aid it in cutting across the grain. The block plane is designed to be held in one hand, but it's all right to use both hands if you're careful.

When through using a plane, adjust the plane iron so that the cutting edge does not stick out past the bottom of the bed and, when you lay a plane down, place it on its side to protect the cutting edge. This will prevent dulling and nicking of the blade. Keep the metal parts oiled when the plane is not in use. And don't let the plane drop. It breaks easily at the throat, which is the slot through which the cutting edge protrudes.

For cutting irregular curves, use the spokeshave or the drawknife. See the section on *Draw Knife*, for further information on both tools.

Planters

If you like to get away from the usual flower pot, and at the same time utilize some interesting receptacles you have in the house, here are a few suggestions.

An old porch light or lantern is an excellent container for growing hanging ivy. It may be suspended from the ceiling, or from a wall bracket.

The unused bird cage is very popular and attractive as a receptacle for small pots of foliage plants with trailing leaves. The pots are placed on the floor of the cage, the leaves come through the wires. The cage may be brass or other metal, and could be left in its former state or painted to harmonize with the decorative scheme of the house. The cage is then hung on a wall bracket, or from the ceiling, or left on its original floor stand.

The outdoor window box which holds the flower pots in the summer can be made to look just as good in the winter months by sticking into the sand some branches of evergreen to give attractiveness to the window during the cold period.

Also see *Flower Boxes*.

Contemporary Planting Boxes

Plastic fiberglass panels can be used to make attractive flower boxes and planters for inside and outside the home. These panels come in different colors and patterns and, when

used for a planter, require no further maintenance.

Here are plans for three different units—a porch planter, a modular planter and a terrace planter.

Photograph and sketches courtesy of
Monsanto Chemical Co.

Materials Needed:

1 piece of 1"x1" aluminum angle
64" long

2 pieces of 1"x1" aluminum angle
11" long

4 pieces of flat plastic fiberglass
6¾"x15¾"

1 piece of flat plastic fiberglass
15¾"x15¾"

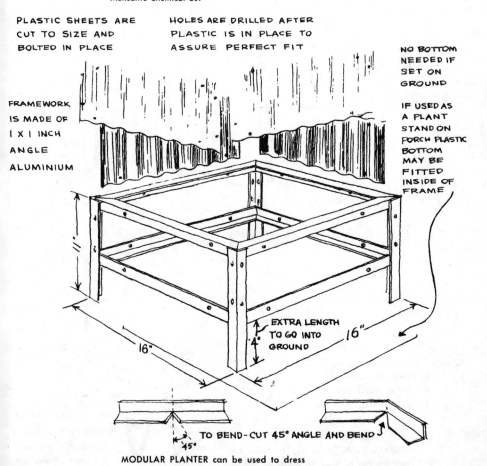

PLASTIC SHEETS ARE
CUT TO SIZE AND
BOLTED IN PLACE

HOLES ARE DRILLED AFTER
PLASTIC IS IN PLACE TO
ASSURE PERFECT FIT

NO BOTTOM
NEEDED IF
SET ON
GROUND

FRAMEWORK
IS MADE OF
1 X 1 INCH
ANGLE
ALUMINIUM

IF USED AS
A PLANT
STAND ON
PORCH PLASTIC
BOTTOM
MAY BE
FITTED
INSIDE OF
FRAME

16"

16"

EXTRA LENGTH
TO GO INTO
GROUND

4"

TO BEND - CUT 45° ANGLE AND BEND

45°

MODULAR PLANTER can be used to dress
up a plain-looking patio or terrace by
spotting these shallow planters where
you want spots of color.

Materials Needed:

2 pieces 18″ long of 2x4
2 pieces 11¾″ long of 2x4
4 pieces 16½″ long of 2x2
6 pieces 18″ long of 1x2
1 piece 7″ long of 1x2
2 pieces 18″ long of 1x2
2 pieces 16½″ long of 1x2

2 pieces 14¾″ long of 1x2
1 piece 7″ long of 1x2
4 pieces of flat plastic fiberglass
   14⅝″x17⅝″
1 piece of flat plastic fiberglass
   14⅝″ square

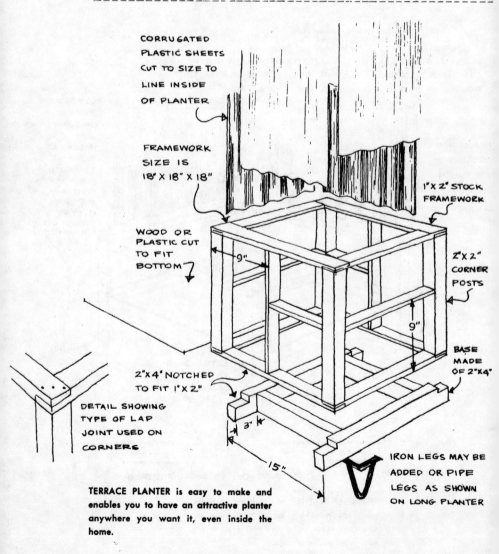

CORRUGATED PLASTIC SHEETS CUT TO SIZE TO LINE INSIDE OF PLANTER

FRAMEWORK SIZE IS 18″ X 18″ X 18″

WOOD OR PLASTIC CUT TO FIT BOTTOM

1″X 2″ STOCK FRAMEWORK

2″X 2″ CORNER POSTS

9″

9″

BASE MADE OF 2″X 4″

2″X 4″ NOTCHED TO FIT 1″X 2″

DETAIL SHOWING TYPE OF LAP JOINT USED ON CORNERS

3″

15″

IRON LEGS MAY BE ADDED OR PIPE LEGS AS SHOWN ON LONG PLANTER

TERRACE PLANTER is easy to make and enables you to have an attractive planter anywhere you want it, even inside the home.

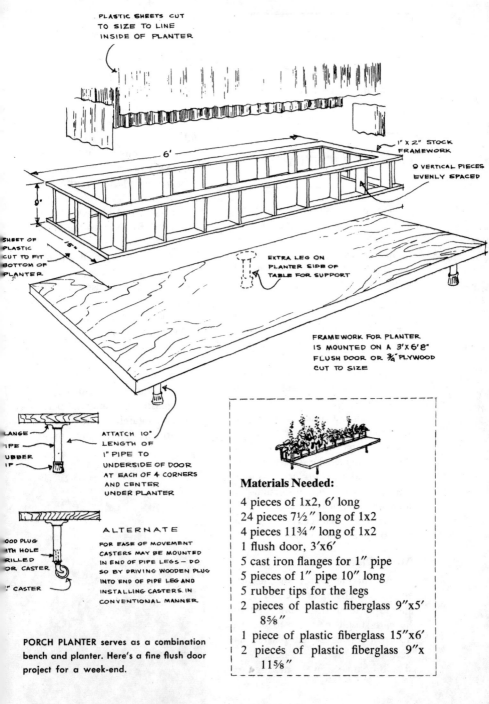

PLASTIC SHEETS CUT
TO SIZE TO LINE
INSIDE OF PLANTER

1" x 2" STOCK
FRAMEWORK

9 VERTICAL PIECES
EVENLY SPACED

6'

9"

15"

SHEET OF
PLASTIC
CUT TO FIT
BOTTOM OF
PLANTER

EXTRA LEG ON
PLANTER SIDE OF
TABLE FOR SUPPORT

FRAMEWORK FOR PLANTER
IS MOUNTED ON A 3'x 6' 8"
FLUSH DOOR OR ¾" PLYWOOD
CUT TO SIZE

FLANGE
PIPE
RUBBER
TIP

ATTATCH 10"
LENGTH OF
1" PIPE TO
UNDERSIDE OF DOOR
AT EACH OF 4 CORNERS
AND CENTER
UNDER PLANTER

WOOD PLUG
WITH HOLE
DRILLED
FOR CASTER

CASTER

ALTERNATE

FOR EASE OF MOVEMENT
CASTERS MAY BE MOUNTED
IN END OF PIPE LEGS — DO
SO BY DRIVING WOODEN PLUG
INTO END OF PIPE LEG AND
INSTALLING CASTERS IN
CONVENTIONAL MANNER

PORCH PLANTER serves as a combination
bench and planter. Here's a fine flush door
project for a week-end.

Materials Needed:

4 pieces of 1x2, 6' long
24 pieces 7½" long of 1x2
4 pieces 11¾" long of 1x2
1 flush door, 3'x6'
5 cast iron flanges for 1" pipe
5 pieces of 1" pipe 10" long
5 rubber tips for the legs
2 pieces of plastic fiberglass 9"x5'
8⅝"
1 piece of plastic fiberglass 15"x6'
2 pieces of plastic fiberglass 9"x
11⅝"

Plants

For different types of plants for inside the home and how to care for them, see section on *Gardening, Indoors*.

For plants and shrubs outdoors, see *Landscaping*.

Plaster

Plaster consists of hardening material mixed with sand or other aggregates, such as vermiculite and perlite, spread evenly over a prepared base while in a soft, workable state. Plaster is noncombustible and, if made of good material properly mixed and applied to a solid base, the resulting surface should be hard and durable. Plaster may be finished in either a smooth or textured surface, to which a choice of decorative treatments may be applied. The most widely used hardening materials are slaked lime, calcined gypsum, and Portland cement. Lime is added to gypsum or Portland cement to make the mixture more workable and to produce a smooth finish, but gypsum and Portland cement should not be mixed together. Good commercial ready-mixed plasters are also available.

Mixing Plaster

All mixing boxes and utensils should be clean, and clean water should be used in the mix. Particular care should be taken to see that no trace of hardened plaster has been left in the mixing box. Water should be placed in the mixing box, and the dry plaster sifted into the water. The mix should be stirred thoroughly to dissolve all lumps and to bring the plaster to the consistency of putty. It can then be picked up on a broad-bladed plastering trowel and forced into the crack or break in the wall.

Where only a small amount of fresh plaster is needed, plaster of Paris alone may be used. Because it hardens so quickly if used without a retarder, only as much as can be put in place within 10 minutes should be mixed at one time.

The addition of small amounts of ordinary glue dissolved in the mixing water will retard the setting of the plaster. Commercial patching plasters containing retarding material are available and may be

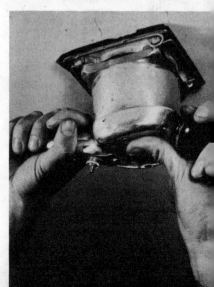

worked for a longer time than the ordinary plaster of Paris. They may also contain other ingredients that improve their working qualities.

The following tools and materials are needed: A small diamond-shaped mason's trowel or broad-bladed putty knife for cracks and small holes; a plasterer's trowel and shallow pan for plastering large areas; plaster of Paris or commercial patching plaster, a small amount of ordinary glue, if necessary, and clean water.

Wall and Ceiling Plastering

To prepare new or unpainted plaster, fill all cracks and holes with patching plaster. Cut out plaster along the crack or around the hole in an inverted V-shape so that edges converge toward the surface. Soak edges with water to bond patching plaster with the existing plaster. Fill the crack to within ¼″ of the surface and allow the patching plaster to set partially before leveling up the wall surface. After cracks and holes have been repaired, smooth rough places with fine sandpaper. Remove loose dirt, dust, or chalky plaster by brushing or washing with clean water. Wash off grease with warm water and mild soap and rinse surface carefully with water. If grease has penetrated deeply, cut out and patch the area affected. Wash only small areas at a time and rinse immediately. If an oil paint is to be applied following plaster repairs, allow the wall to dry for at least 72 hours.

Plaster Repairs

For instructions on how to mend

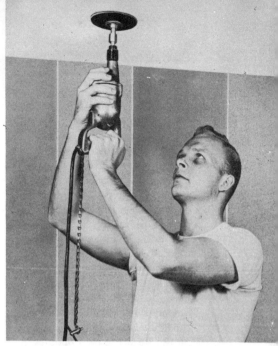

cracks and breaks in plaster refer to the section on *Ceiling Repairs*.

Painting

Whenever possible, let new plaster age or cure before painting, especially if oil paint is to be applied. If painting must be before plaster ages, use calcimine, cold-water paint, or resin-emulsion paint. Or you can cure the plaster, removing the free lime by washing the surface with a solution of 3½ lbs. of zinc sulphate crystals mixed in 1 gallon of water. Dust the surface when dry; leave for at least another 24 hours before painting.

Also see *Painting, Interior*.

Repainting

The condition of the plaster surfaces to be repainted largely determines the number of coats needed. Repeated painting builds up film thickness and leads to paint failure. With surfaces properly cleaned and prepared, one coat may be sufficient.

1. *Cleaning surface*—When the wall surface is in good condition and painted with casein, resin-emulsion, or a flat paint, the only preparation necessary is to clean the surface by brushing or wiping with turpentine or mineral spirits. For dirty or greasy surfaces such as kitchen walls and ceilings, apply a preparation made by adding to warm water a small amount of detergent and sufficient flour or paperhanger's paste to make a slightly sticky mixture. Spread this mixture with a large calcimine brush, allow it to remain on the surface 2 or 3 minutes, and wash it off with a sponge or cloth and clean water.

2. *Removing old paint*—Wash off the calcimine coating before applying another type of paint. Oil paint can be applied over casein or resin-emulsion paint in sound condition if there are no more than two coats of old paint on the surface. Remove all loose, scaling, or flaking paint by scraping or wire brushing. Sandpaper the edges which have been scraped. Do not remove the entire coat if only a small area has deteriorated.

3. *Removing resin-emulsion paint, flat wall paint, and enamels*—To remove resin-emulsion paint, flat wall paint, and enamels, use paint-and-varnish remover. Brush on the remover and scrape or wipe off the softened paint. To remove paraffin left on the surface by some types of removers, wash walls with mineral spirits, or commercial wall cleaner and warm water.

4. *Removing casein paints*—To remove casein paint, scrub wall with a strong solution of trisodium phosphate and hot water, using a stiff brush. Rinse surface thoroughly with clean water and allow it to dry before repainting.

5. *Retouching surface*—After loose paint has been removed or the wall surface has been cleaned, fill all crack and holes with patching plaster or spackling compound. To patch areas larger than 1 sq. ft., use hydrated lime and gaging plaster. Spot-paint the patched areas before applying a new coat.

Plaster Walls

Have you always shied away from plastering a wall? Do you think of it as a job only for a man with long experience? Then listen to this:

Any able amateur can put up modern plaster walls—the type you find in hundreds of new homes. What's more, these walls can be put on right over an old surface, without tearing down old plaster.

It's true that a slick, three-coat plaster job is just as difficult to achieve as ever, and, if you must have that, better hire a professional. What you can do yourself is simply skip the difficult part—the final white coat that must be troweled glass-smooth. By letting two coats do the work of three, you end up with an intentionally textured surface.

New plaster over old is latest trick for repairing damaged wall without tearing it down. Lath is nailed over old wall, then covered with new lightweight plaster that adds modern, textured finish without extra work and weight of old-type plaster job.

If you prefer plaster board, you can also achieve a finish that looks like textured plaster. You do it with new plaster like paints.

Wall on a wall—One of the developments that makes it easier to put new plaster on an old wall is a dimpled metal lath that has a series of small depressions pressed into it. These hold the lath about ¼" away from the wall so that plaster can get in behind, and save the need for furring strips.

Another development that helps is the development of new lightweight plasters which can be put over an existing wall without overloading the structural members. These come premixed like cake batter and need only water to make them ready to use. Containing extremely light aggregates such as perlite or vermiculite, they weigh only half as much as regular sanded plaster. They're sold under a variety of trade names, but you can be sure of getting the right type if you ask for them by name.

How-To

The lath comes in strips about 26″ wide and 8′ long. The only trick in putting it up is to make sure that it is nailed firmly to the studs through the old wall. You can find the studs, usually 16″ between centers, by tapping the wall or drilling test holes that will be covered with plaster later. Mark the studs with a heavy colored crayon that will show through the lath. All lath strips must start and end on studs to insure a firm bond with the wall.

With the lath up, the first or "scratch" coat is troweled on just deep enough to cover the lath. The second or "brown" coat should then be put on before the first has completely dried, usually the following day. If you have to wait longer, wet down the first coat before applying the second. The final smoothing of the second coat produces a sand finish that can be left as is or further textured with one of the special paints.

Plasterboard

On new walls, you'll probably find it easier to put up your plaster in the form of big plasterboard sheets. These are 4′ wide and come in lengths up to 12′. The 4′x8′ size,

Lathing the Wall

1. Casing beads, made of metal channel with narrow strips of lath attached, are first nailed around windows and doors to frame openings and form "grounds" to guide depth of plaster. Use hacksaw and miter corners to a close fit.

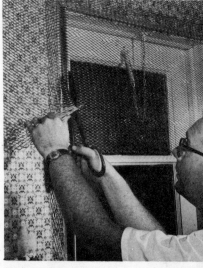

2. Lath is nailed to studs through old wall. Run strips across windows and other openings, then trim out waste. Use 2″ roofing nails about 8″ apart. Overlap strips 2″ at edges and stagger end joints so they fall on different studs.

3. At corners, bend lath around 2x4 and tap into place to make neat, sharp angle. Make sure end turning corner is long enough to reach next nearest stud. For outside corners, special metal bead is nailed over edge first.

4. Openings for outlets are cut after lath is put up. Fixtures must be set out ¾" to bring them flush with the plaster. This can be done with extension rings, made to fit most outlet boxes, or by blocking box out with wood from behind.

5. New picture molding is slotted metal strip that's nailed to wall 8" to 10" below ceiling after lath is in place. Strip provides almost invisible groove for hanging pictures without nailing into plaster and also serves as upper grounds, or guide line, for gauging thickness of plaster. At the same time, a ¾"-thick wood strip several inches wide is nailed along base of wall to form lower grounds. Strip also provides nailing surface for fastening on baseboard later.

1. First plaster coat is troweled on just thick enough to embed lath completely. Work plaster in and around lath to insure firm bond. Mix plaster to a stiff, buttery consistency and work quickly, as it sets in about an hour.

2. Scratch marks are made as first coat begins to set but is still workable. Use scrap piece of lath and make crisscross furrows in plaster to roughen it and provide good gripping surface for second, or "brown", plaster coat.

Two-Coat Plaster Technique

3. Second coat is put on slightly thicker than needed, then scraped down flush with grounds with 1x6" board that rides on picture molding at top and wood strip at bottom. Low spots are filled, rough areas smoothed.

4. Wood float gives final finish to second coat. Let plaster dry firm but not hard, then rub float over face with flat, circular motion. Result is smooth, sandy texture that makes attractive finish without further work.

however, is about the limit for easy handling by one person and just fits nicely across three stud spaces when put up vertically or six stud spaces horizontally.

The more common thickness is ⅜″, but the ½″ will give you a more solid wall at only slight extra cost. Be sure also to get the recessed-edge type. These panels form a shallow depression along each joint into which you cement a special patching tape to provide a smooth, flush seam.

The finished wall can be textured in any one of the several ways shown to hide nails and joints, or can be wallpapered. If you're going to paper, be sure to prime the wall first with varnish, or the wallpaper will stick so firmly to the paper face of the plasterboard that you'll never be able to remove it without damaging the wall.

1. Running sheets crosswise gives greater strength, fewer seams. Start panels at top of wall. Use broad-head wallboard nails, spaced 5″ to 7″ apart. Countersink each nailhead slightly to make hollow for patching cement.

Putting Up Plasterboard

2. Sheets are trimmed with any sharp knife. Run knife along straightedge to score top face of panel and snap piece down to break core. Then score bottom face and snap piece back up, and it will break off cleanly.

3. To conceal joints, first fill seams with patching cement, then press perforated tape firmly into cement with wide-blade putty knife as shown. Add enough more cement to embed tape fully and smooth out edges with blade.

4. Second coat of cement is applied to seam after first coat has dried. A wide plasterer's trowel is ideal for this. Feather edges out 6" to 8" on each side of tape to blend with wall. Fill all nailheads flush with face of panels.

5. Ceiling joints are covered in same way as other seams except that tape is first creased down middle to firm angle that fits in corner. For smoothest appearance, seams and nailheads should be sanded after cement is dry.

6. New corner beads have metal reinforcements on back side of tape, making strong joints that won't chip or crack if accidentally bumped. Beads come for inside and outside corners (inset), are cemented like regular tape.

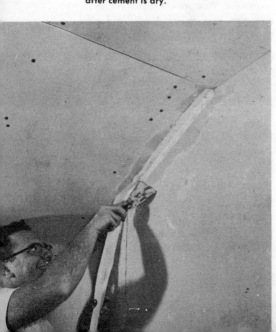

Textured Paint

The new textured paints are thick, pastelike compounds that look more like plaster and give similar results. They come in a variety of colors and in water-, rubber-, and oil-base types.

Simply brushed on and allowed to dry, these paints form a hard, sandlike finish that hides blemishes in both plaster and plasterboard. Or you can handle the paint in various way to get different textures as shown in the photos.

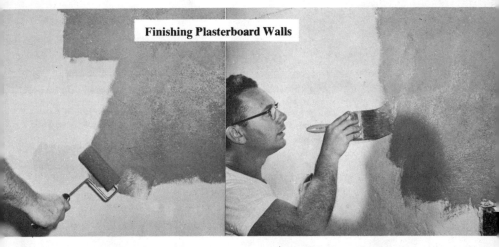

Finishing Plasterboard Walls

1. Thick, pastelike textured paint easily hides seams and nailheads in plasterboard even when not sanded smooth, as here. Using roller helps spread paint evenly, provides slight stipple effect that can be left as is.

2. Over plaster wall, textured paint fills in small holes and trowel marks, giving surface a smoother appearance. Paint is worked into plaster with brush, and can then be left as is for sand finish or given a texture.

3. Paint can be textured on either plaster or plasterboard walls in several easy ways as shown. You can get a heavy, stucco-like stipple by simply daubing paint with sponge after thick coat has been brushed on (left). Modern striated effect is obtained with wide-tooth hair comb (center). Wavy lines can be made by twisting comb as you move it along. Swirls and other freehand designs can be made by twisting a stiff-bristled brush (right).

New glue-on panels are cemented to wall instead of nailed, eliminating fuss of patching seams and nailheads. They can be put right up over old walls or over a backing of regular plasterboard in new walls.

Cement is applied with special notched spreader that leaves three ribbons on back of panel (left). Panel is then pressed into wall and tamped tightly against preceding panel with 2x4 (right). Panels come white for painting or in colors.

Plastic Fiberglas

Plastic fiberglas is widely used as roofing over a patio or terrace.

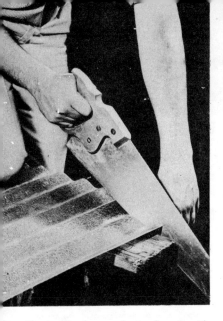

Plastic fiberglas panels can be cut with an ordinary hand saw or with an abrasive wheel on a power saw.

Flat plastic fiberglas can also be cut with metal shears.

Photographs courtesy of Alsynite Company of America.

Reinforced plastic fiberglas panels have many uses inside and outside the home. They are available in:

- many different colors—white, blue, green, etc.
- translucent or opaque
- flat sheets, steplap or
- corrugated panels, with corrugations of 1¼″, 2½″, 2.67″ and 4.2″
- varying widths from about 26″ to 40″, depending upon the make
- in lengths from about 1′ to 13′ or even larger on special order.

This plastic can be worked easily by the homeowner. It is extremely durable but also very light in weight. Furthermore, it is weather-proof, fire-resistant and practically color-fast. Once installed, it requires no further maintenance.

Although widely used for roofing over patios and terraces, plastic

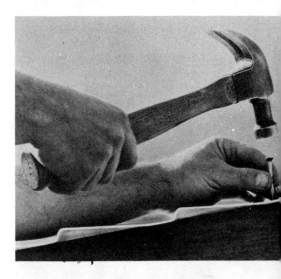

These plastic panels can be fastened with screws, nuts and bolts and nails. When using nails for a roof out-of-doors, use special roofing nails with a neoprene washer under the head. It is best to pre-drill the plastic for the nail or screw to prevent crazing of the fiberglas.

Corrugated plastic panels are easily curved to form a wall conforming to the contour of the pool.

Photograph courtesy of Filon Industries, Inc.

Reinforced Fiberglas plastic top is used as a top surface for this floor fan unit made by Vornado.

Photograph courtesy of Owens-Corning Fiberglas Corp.

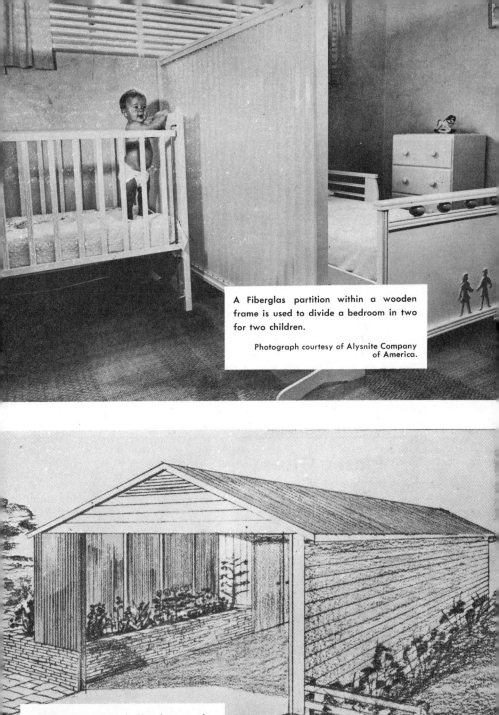

A Fiberglas partition within a wooden frame is used to divide a bedroom in two for two children.

Photograph courtesy of Alysnite Company of America.

Reinforced corrugated fiberglas can be used for roofs as well as walls in garages and other buildings.

Sketch courtesy of Monsanto Chemical Corp.

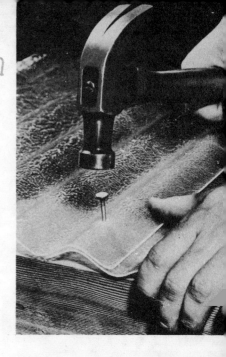

fiberglas can also be used for planters, front door canopy, awnings, room divider panels, roofs over garages and carports, walls for carports and garages, doors for shower enclosures, fences, and as ceilings inside the home as well as many other uses. Because it is thin and strong it is easily curved without breaking.

When two panels are joined side by side, there should be an overlap of the corrugations. A lap of anywhere from one to two full corrugations is necessary depending upon the pitch of the corrugation and the turn of the side. Using a special mastic between the two panels will produce a waterproof seam.

Photographs courtesy of Alsynite Company of America.

Plastic Glass

Fiberglass cloth combined with plastic resins are used to produce new surfaces. Available in kit form —fiberglass cloth, epoxy resins and hardeners—plastic glass can be used to patch holes in metal (it works perfectly on cars) as well as other surfaces. The kits come with complete instructions for use, varying to some extent depending upon the chemical formulation.

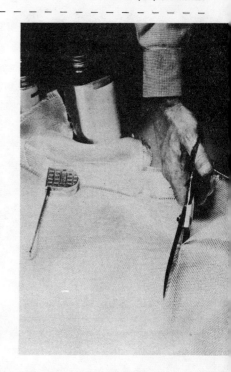

Fiberglass cloth combined with plastic resins and hardeners are used to produce new surfaces and are particularly useful for patching holes in metal.

Plastic Laminates

Various materials surfaced with melamine resin under heat and pressure are called plastic laminates. Some people call these materials "Formica," but this is a registered trade mark. Some of the other plastic laminates are Micarta, Consoweld, Naugatop, Conolite, etc.

Plastic laminates are available in solid colors, patterns and wood. The solid colors and patterns are printed paper with a protective melamine surface. Some of the wood grains are also printed on paper but others are real wood, about 1/64" thick, protected by the plastic surface.

For details about working with plastic laminates, see *Laminates, Counter Tops* and *Furniture Finishing.*

Easy-to-clean, durable plastic laminates can be used to refinish old furniture; merely glue the Formica in place. See **Counter Tops.**

Photograph courtesy of The Formica Co.

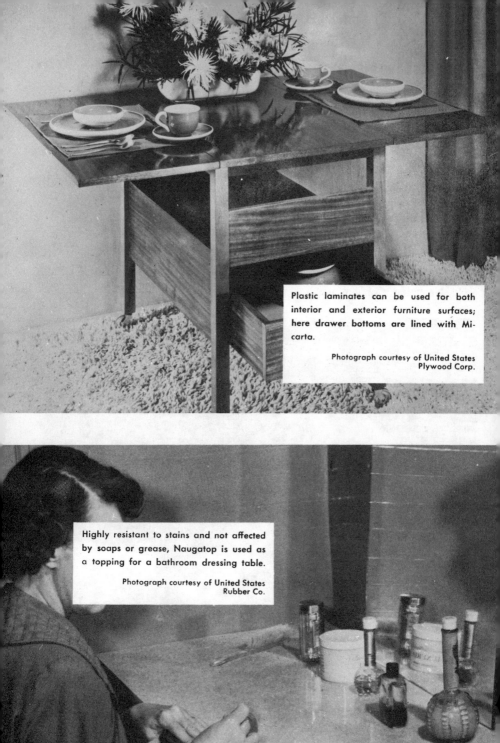

Plastic laminates can be used for both interior and exterior furniture surfaces; here drawer bottoms are lined with Micarta.

Photograph courtesy of United States Plywood Corp.

Highly resistant to stains and not affected by soaps or grease, Naugatop is used as a topping for a bathroom dressing table.

Photograph courtesy of United States Rubber Co.

Plastic Pipe

Home plumbing jobs have always required a bit of know-how, and always will, but flexible plastic pipe makes them a lot easier. If you have a plumbing job coming up, this tough lightweight material may save time and money.

If you have dreamed of an underground lawn sprinkler system, plastic pipe is just right. No need to worry about freezing, for ice just stretches the pipe a bit. For the man who wants to tie a new outdoor hose connection, a home darkroom, or a water softener into the house cold-water system, plastic pipe does away with the problem of pipe cutters and threading tools needed to bring metal pipe around basement obstructions. It bends easily around curves, and any saw or sharp knife will cut it.

What is it?—Technically, plastic pipe is extruded polyethylene or

Saw or knife will cut plastic pipe. No need for a special tool, and no reaming is needed after the cut.

vinyl. It weighs about one-eighth of the equivalent metal pipe, comes in standard pipe dimensions in coils containing up to 400 unbroken feet, and is absolutely inert with respect to drinking water and a long list of solutions and chemicals.

For the home user, the last point

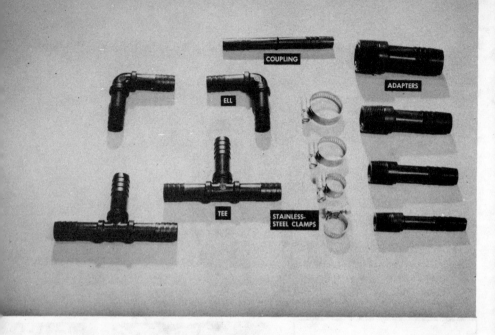

COUPLING

ELL

ADAPTERS

TEE

STAINLESS-STEEL CLAMPS

Special fittings are made of rigid plastic. Stainless-steel clamps draw plastic pipe down on serrated ends of fittings, making leakproof connections. Fittings with threaded ends permit connections to standard pipe fittings. Other fittings include reducers and plugs all matched to standard pipe threads.

means no "pipe" taste in the water, and, even more important, less likelihood of expensive replacement jobs in the course of time. With plastic pipe, rust, scale and electrolytic corrosion just don't occur. Connections, either into conventional metal pipe or plastic-to-plastic, are made with molded hard-plastic fittings that are forced into the ends of the pipe and held permanently by stainless-steel clamps. Plastic to metal fittings have standard pipe threads on one end for ease in making the joint.

Not for hot water—Plastic pipe at present can't be used for steam lines, or where water temperatures may exceed 160°F. This usually rules it out for domestic hot-water lines, unless it can be made certain that the water heater will never deliver temperatures above this point.

And while automatic water heaters are often set at 135° or 140°, the below-160° restriction could be a handicap with future dish- and clothes-washers, which sometimes require very hot water.

Since plastic pipe suffers some ill effects from prolonged exposure to direct sunlight, it should be covered at least lightly when installed outdoors. It does not deteriorate underground.

Although the pipe will merely expand when water freezes inside it, alternate freezing and thawing eventually may burst it. Plastic pipe, incidentally, can't be thawed by an arc welder since it is not a conductor.

Will it do your job?—Answering this won't take much thought. Tests have shown that bursting pressures range from 540 lb. per square inch for ½″ pipe to 200 lb. for 1¼″ pipe, about as small and as large as pipe comes in most houses. Normal city or well-pump pressures don't come anywhere near these values. Since the pipe stays flexible to minus 40°F. and lower, you haven't any worries on that score. Laboratory tests indicate a working life of easily 30 years.

How much?—Plastic pipe costs less than copper tubing, about the same as galvanized metal, and, if its flexibility and easy go-together permit you to do the job yourself, you'll save the cost of professional cutting, reaming, threading, and wrench pulling.

Even though it isn't recommended for hot-water systems, plastic pipe has been found to be practical for radiant heating because it is jointless and easily formed into the necessary loops and coils. Here, as long as temperatures are kept below 160°F., all is well.

It's ideal for wells.—One job where plastic pipe reigns supreme is on a jet-well installation. Anyone who has tried to juggle a jet on the end of a double length of heavy pipe, lower it into a casing, and hold it while new pipe sections are upended and threaded into what is hoped will be a leakproof coupling, knows how difficult it is. Pulling the pipe to make repairs is even worse.

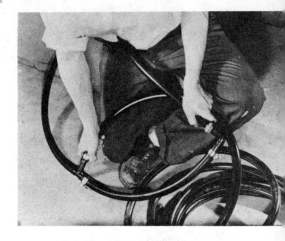

It bends easily. One of the conveniences of plastic pipe is the ease of assembling complex hookups. This assembly was clamped to ceiling of home darkroom.

Home appliances like this water softener can be hooked up in minutes with plastic pipe. Persons living in rented property and owning the appliances can therefore move them.

Jet-well hookup is easier with plastic pipe. Insert adapters; join the two lengths of plastic pipe to the jet. Threaded connections here are sealed with Permatex No. 2. Other standard pipe dopes are not recommended on plastic fittings. After jet is connected, the pipes slide easily down the casing. Well casing also is now being made of hard plastic.

particularly if the pipe joints are rusted solid.

All too frequently in metal pipe, high friction and scale team up to throttle pump output way below capacity. Naturally, the over-worked pump has a shortened life. Plastic pipe, weighing only eight lbs. for every 100 lb. of metal pipe, makes the whole job simple. The jet is coupled to the pipe, the whole assembly is poked down the casing to the desired depth without a hoist, and the upper ends are sawed off and coupled to the pump.

If the well gives trouble later, the plastic pipe can be pulled out intact—regardless of whether a structure has been built over the well. Jet pump installations may go as deep as 150 to 200 feet. The exact limits are established as the depth

Lengths of plastic pipe are joined by clamping their ends on notched ends of an insert coupling or, as in photo, a T. A sealer is not needed to make joints watertight.

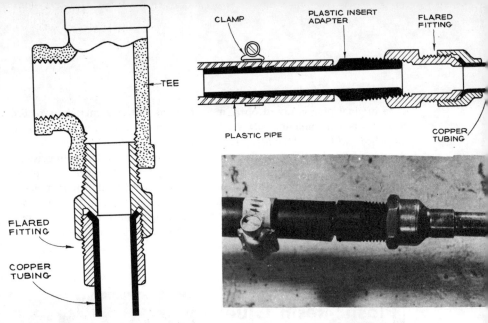

Copper tubing can be joined to plastic pipe with either flared or sweated fittings. The sketches show two uses of flared fittings. The photo shows how a sweated-on female connection can be used to receive the male threads of a plastic insert adapted.

where the combined water head plus the pumping pressure does not exceed the recommended working pressure of the pipe.

New connections are easy.— Still another advantage to the user comes when the pipe must go into a trench. A plow furrow often suffices. Since straightness is not important, the pipe can be snaked around where it is wanted without regard for the limiting angles of conventional pipe fittings.

At a later time, if it is desired to intercept the original pipe with a take-off to another pipe line, no excavation of full pipe lengths for cutting and threading is required.

Metal to plastic pipe connections require no plumbing know-how. In photo, a metal coupling receives male threads of galvanized pipe and the hard plastic insert adapter. Plastic pipe is then slipped over end of adapter and clamp tightened.

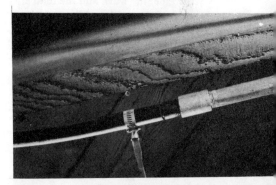

Hard plastic T's and elbows also help make joints easy. Plastic pipe plugs are available, but a metal one as shown here will work.

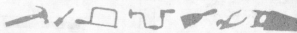

The original pipe is sawed open, a tee clamped in, and the new lead attached without difficulty. This feature makes plastic pipe attractive to cities for gas and water service leads, and to the farmer with plans which will require future taps into the main line.

From the insurance standpoint, the material is classified as "slow-burning." It is a matter of record that plastic pipe in a Texas manufacturing plant did burn through and release its water, extinguishing a fire that threatened the plant. From this, it would seem that plastic pipe carrying water through your home might also serve as a thermo-triggered sprinkler system.

Plastic-Resin Glue

This is used for woodworking joints, veneering and repairing wood furniture. The glue, of urea-resin type, is strong, slow setting, easy to use. It is water-resistant, durable and does not stain the wood. It comes in powder form, and mixing directions are on the package. For best results the glue, the work and the temperature of the room, while the glue is setting, should be 70° F. or higher. The package must be kept tightly sealed when not in use.

See *Adhesives*.

Plastic resin glue must be used with clamps. Don't forget to use protective pieces to protect work from clamp jaws.

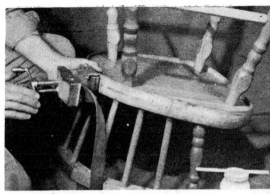

Edge gluing of new plywood tape as well as wood veneers can be applied with plastic resin glue.

When plastic resin glue is used on curved surfaces, it can be clamped with a band clamp.

Instead of clamps with the glue, you can use special glass filament tape to hold the legs.

Another "clamping" technique is to use rope to hold the legs of a chair while the glue is drying.

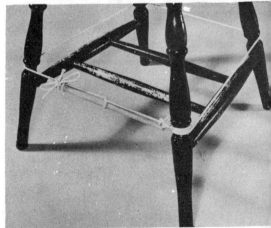

Plastic Wall Tiles

For full details on how to install plastic wall tiles, refer to section on *Tiles*.

Plastic wall tiles are easy to install.

Photographs courtesy of Tilemaster Corp.

To conceal the wall-floor joint, special cove tiles can be cemented in place.

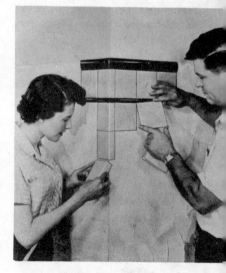

To go around corners with plastic wall tile, use special molded corner tiles.

Plastic Wood

"Plastic Wood" is the registered trade name of a special wood filler. See *Crack Fillers* and *Wood Fillers*.

Play Equipment for Children

Photograph courtesy of Armstrong Cork Co.

Attractive child's room provides adequate play space for the youngster. Note the easy-to-make shelves for storing toys and books (see **Built-Ins** for how-to informa- tion), combination perforated hardboard bulletin board and blackboard on the wall. Easy-to-clean and skid-proof vinyl-asbestos tile on floor makes fine play area.

Some simple home-made play apparatus is needed in every back yard where children play. A few smooth boards of different widths, lengths, and thicknesses, not too heavy for a little child to carry, can be used for building and climbing Large blocks made like hollow wooden boxes are useful for push- ing and climbing. Wooden packing

boxes of different sizes, from which the extra nails have been pulled so that the children can safely climb into the boxes, are material for playing house or store or for other imaginative play. A major appliance container or any other large box with windows cut in the sides makes a good playhouse.

A work table can be used outdoors as well as in the playroom. The work table for children 4 to 6 should be equipped with durable and efficient tools, such as a hammer with a short handle and broad head; a small vise; a short, wide saw; and short galvanized nails with large flat heads (roofing nails). There should be plenty of wood to work with—wood that is soft enough for the small child to saw easily and to drive nails into.

Sand Box

To make a box large enough for two or three children to play in, you need this materal:

Sides: 2 pieces of 2x10 lumber, 6' long.

Ends: 2 pieces of 2x10 lumber, 4' long.

Shelves: 2 pieces of 2x8 lumber, 4' 4" long.

Nails: 1 lb. 16d common.

Sand: 1 wagonload (to fill the box to a depth of 8", approximately ½ cu. yd. or 16 cu. ft. of sand will be required).

To construct, nail the side boards to the ends. Center the boards for the shelves on the end boards and nail them firmly to both end and side boards, so that they are half inside and half outside the box and will not need to be braced. Cut off the sharp corners of the shelves. Brace the corners of the box with iron or wood. A wooden bottom in the sand box will keep the children from digging into the soil underneath and mixing it with the sand.

Any sound grade of softwood lumber can be used for the sand box. Among the low-priced woods

Easy-to-build sand box.

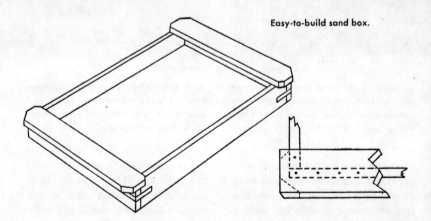

are pine, fir, and spruce. The boards should be free from knotholes and other defects through which sand can sift readily. One-inch lumber may be used if stakes are driven into the ground at intervals to hold

Play ladder for younger children is propped up on one end only.

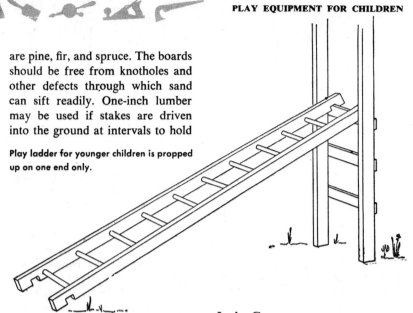

the boards in place. No. 1 and No. 2 Common grades of lumber will be satisfactory for a sand box. Smooth boards should be selected, and the top edges of the boards, inside and outside, should be smoothed with a plane or a wood rasp and sandpaper.

The sand box should have a cover to protect the sand from stray cats and dogs. Canvas weighted at the corners with stones may be used, or wallboard nailed on two strips of wood may be laid over the sand box at night. Another type of cover is a light wooden frame covered with 1″ galvanized-wire mesh, which permits the sun and air to reach the sand. To keep the sand dry in wet weather, however, a permanent cover, hinged to the box, is best. It may be made of waterproof canvas or other fabric stretched and nailed to a frame, or of wood, or of wallboard and wood. Both wood and wallboard should be painted with waterproof paint.

Junior Gym

Junior gym, for tots from one to three years old, calls for plywood, half-round molding and 1⅝″ pine stock. Its independently constructed ladder, ramp and step sections can be set up in several different ways, or moved indoors to keep the children busy on rainy days.

Smooth all parts with sandpaper, slightly. Finish the gym with several coats of high-gloss, light-colored enamel.

Basketball Backboard

Basketball backboard that must be mounted on a garage with a sloping roof is easy to build from ¾″ exterior plywood and 2x4's. The frames that hold the backboard upright are bolted together as shown in the drawing. The bolts at the forward end pass through the backboard, while those at the rear pass through the roofing and rafters. Apply roofing compound to the rear bolts before inserting them in the

holes in the roof, and also around commercial basket, or make your own by welding a ring of ⅜″ steel rod to a bracket. The backboard can be modified to be secured to a 1½″ diameter pipe and set into concrete on the ground.

Sand Box Cover

This folding sandbox cover serves a double purpose. During play hours it offers comfortable shade; when the box is not in use, you can fold the legs and set the roof directly on the box to keep the sand clean and dry, and to protect grit-covered toys which don't belong indoors.

When the legs are straightened, pockets formed by cleats on the sandbox sides hold them firmly upright. At the same time, the roof is stiffened by butting cross members attached to the legs. Stretch canvas over the frame, tacking it along the ridgepole and all four sides.

Play Plank and Sawhorse

The material needed, and the construction of the play plank, is as follows:

Plank: 1 piece of vertical-grained fir or pine, 2x10, 12′ long. (Maple or birch, 1¼″ thick, in "clear" or "select" grade, may be used.)

Cleats: 2 pieces of lumber, 4x12 (or double 2x12), 10″ long.

Bolt a cleat to the bottom of the plank 6″ from each end. This is to keep the plank from slipping when it is placed on boxes or on the sawhorse.

Place the play plank across the sawhorse to make a seesaw. Or put it on 2 blocks of wood or on 2 boxes to make a walking board for the child to practice balancing.

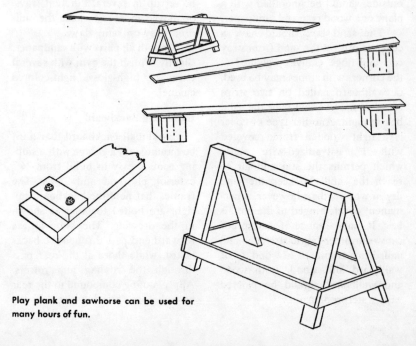

Play plank and sawhorse can be used for many hours of fun.

For the sawhorse, the needed materials and construction are:

Top and legs: 1 piece 2x4 fir or pine, 9' long.

Braces: 1 piece of 1x4 lumber, 6½' long.

Nails: 1 lb. 16d common nails or carriage bolts.

Saw the long piece of lumber as follows: top, 24" long, and 4 legs, each 20" long. At a distance of 6" from each end of the top, bolt two small blocks of wood or saw out a section ¾" deep, to keep the play plank from slipping off the sawhorse. Saw the shorter piece of lumber into four pieces to be used as braces, two 24", two 15". Assemble the pieces and nail the sawhorse together.

Swings and Climbing Bars

For the frame, use fir or pine. The materials needed and construction are:

Uprights for swing: 2 pieces of 4x4 lumber, 14' long.

Cross beam for swing: 1 piece of 4x4 lumber, 6' long.

Upright for climbing bars: 1 piece of 4x4 lumber, 10' long.

Braces: 4 pieces of 2x4 lumber, 8' long (not required if uprights are set 3' in concrete).

Nails: 1 lb. 20d common nails and 1 lb. 7" heavy nails or bolts.

(Note.—The frame may be made of 3" pipe of approximately the same lengths as the lumber.)

Unless specially treated lumber is bought for the uprights, the parts to be placed underground should be treated to a point 6" above the ground to prevent decay or damage from insects.

Fasten the cross beam to the tops of the uprights for the swing with heavy bolts or nails. Square the beam and posts with a carpenter's level or a wide-board that has been cut square. Brace the angles (joints) of the cross beam and uprights securely with wood or iron. Dig three post holes for the uprights 3' deep. Center the two post holes for the swing uprights 6' apart. The post hole for the other upright, to support the climbing bars, should be 4' from the upright for the swing. Make square forms for the holes. Set the uprights on pieces of wood so that they will be level. Rough, ready-made wooden boxes to fit the holes may be used as forms for the concrete. The uprights will not need permanent braces if they are set 3' deep in concrete. They must be braced temporarily, however, until the concrete is set.

A proportion of water to cement that would give adequate strength in concrete foundations for playground equipment is 6 gallons of water to 1 sack of Portland cement. If the maximum screening size of the gravel is 1" the proportions may be 1 part of cement, 2 parts of sand, and 3 parts of gravel. If the maximum size of the gravel is 2", the proportions may be 1 part of cement, 2 parts of sand, and 3½ parts of gravel. The exact amount of sand and gravel necessary to make the mixture workable may be determined by mixing trial batches. See *Concrete.*

For the swing, the required materials and construction are:

Rope: Waterproof manila rope, ¾" in diameter and about 25' long.

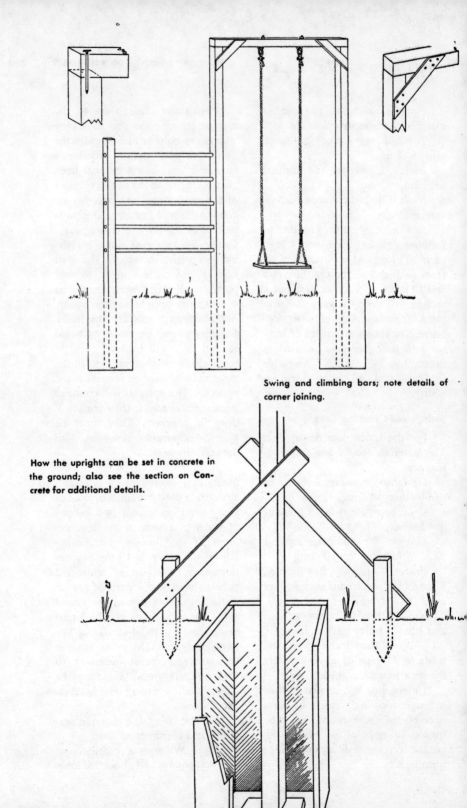

Swing and climbing bars; note details of corner joining.

How the uprights can be set in concrete in the ground; also see the section on Concrete for additional details.

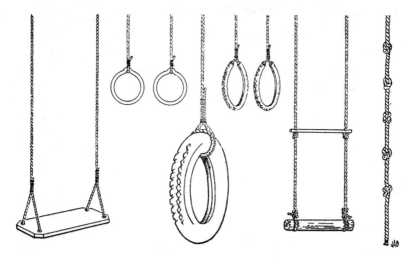

Swing seat ideas.

Swing seat: 1 piece of 1¼x8 maple or birch, 24″ long.

Other kinds of swings require the following material:

1 pair of galvanized steel or aluminum rings 1″ thick and 8″ in diameter.

1 automobile tire.

1 pair of rings made of rubber hose or bicycle tires.

1 piece of log 21″ long and 5″ in diameter, and a balancing rung of oak, ash, or hickory, 21″ long and 1¼″ in diameter, for standing-log swing.

Rope for climbing, 2″ in diameter and approximately 14′ long.

The safest method of constructing the swing is to use special metal fittings such as a 6″ hooked bolt to attach the rope to the cross beam; a galvanized thimble through the hook to prevent wear on the rope; and a clamp to fasten the rope. If a bolt cannot be bought already hooked, bend a heavy, threaded bolt into a J-shaped hook, and put the thimble through the hooked end of the bolt. Bore a hole through the cross beam.

Put the threaded end of the bolt up through the hole in the cross beam and fasten the nut with a wrench, using a washer against the wood. As the bolt is screwed into the cross beam, the hooked end will be forced into the wood so that it cannot pull loose.

Pull one end of the rope through the hook so that the rope rests on the thimble, and fasten the end of the rope with the black enameled clamp. A bowline knot may be used, but the clamp is a more permanent means of fastening the rope to the cross beam.

The swing seat should be low enough for the small child to touch the ground with his whole foot, about 12″ from the ground. For older children, 20″ or 22″ is the usual height.

For the small child it is better to drill four holes in the swing seat, one in each corner, and run the rope through the holes. Round the corners of the swing seat. Put the rope through the holes in the swing seat and fasten by wrapping the ends tightly to the rope with marline (a cord that can be bought at a hardware store or a marine supply house). See sketch showing how to tie and splice rope.

Galvanized wire is often used to wrap rope, but the ends must be fastened carefully and inspected often to prevent the child's getting scratched. The kind of clamp that is used to fasten the rope to the cross beam cannot be used here, because children might get hurt on the metal end.

An effective way of fastening the rope to the hook in the cross beam and to the swing seat is to splice the rope. Usually the company that sells the rope will do the splicing. If this method is used, however, the swing cannot be adjusted to different heights.

The swing may be a standing log swing designed to develop the arches of the feet, or a pair of flying rings for strengthening arm and shoulder muscles. For the small child, rings made of rubber hose or bicycle tires slipped over the rope and fastened tightly will serve very well, but the older, more active child will need metal rings, as the hands will not slip on rubber easily enough for a comfortable change of grip.

An automobile tire swing is popular and can be used in many ways. A casing from which the inner tube and valve have been removed is firmly fastened to a single rope. A used tire is satisfactory, if it is not worn through and the fabric is not thin.

The climbing rope is a heavy single rope in which knots are tied,

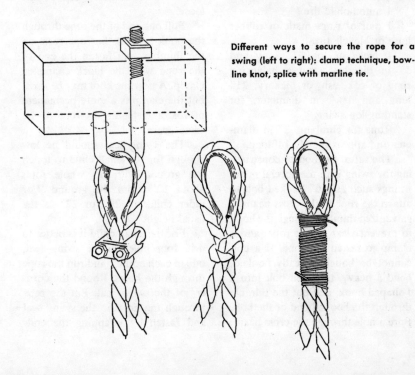

Different ways to secure the rope for a swing (left to right): clamp technique, bowline knot, splice with marline tie.

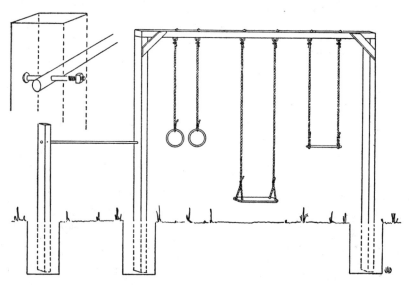

Swing, rings, trapeze and bar arrangement for outdoor fun for the youngsters.

9″ to 14″ apart, the distance depending upon the size of the child who is to use the rope.

For the climbing bars, you need 5 straight-grained maple, hickory, or birch bars, 1¼″ in diameter, 4′ long.

The bars can be bought, finished, from a lumber company or a planing mill. Bore holes 1¼″ in diameter, 12″ apart, in both uprights of the frame. Sandpaper the holes enough to permit the bars to enter. Drive the bars through the holes with a heavy block of wood and a hammer. The bars should fit in the holes so tightly that they cannot slip out or turn in the child's hands.

The climbing bars will be enjoyed by children under 5. One end of the play plank may be placed on one of the lower bars and the other end on the ground or on a box for a walking or bouncing plank. One end of the plank may be placed on a higher bar to make a slide. The cleat on the sliding plank will prevent its slipping.

When the child is older, the wooden bars may be removed by sawing them off close to the upright, and a piece of 1″ pipe placed through the upright for a horizontal bar. This bar should be 1″ or 2″ higher than the child's extended finger tips and should be bolted to the uprights. This may be done by boring holes 7/16″ in diameter bored through the pipe 2″ from each end. Bore a 1½″ hole in each upright through which to place the pipe; then at right angles to the first hole in each upright bore another hole 7/16″ in diameter, exactly intersecting the first hole at the center. Put the bar in place and bolt it with 3/8″ carriage bolts and washers through upright and bar.

Swing, Rings, Trapeze, Bar

Use fir or pine; lumber and other materials needed for the frame are:

Uprights for swing: 2 pieces of 4x6 lumber, 14' long.

Cross beam for swing: 1 piece of 4x6 lumber, 14" long.

Upright for horizontal bar: 1 piece of 4x6 lumber, 9' long.

Braces: 4 pieces of 2x4 lumber. 10' long (not required if uprights are set 3' in concrete).

Nails: 1 lb. 20d common nails or carriage bolts.

(Note.—The frame may be made of 3" pipe of approximately the same lengths as the lumber.)

To construct the frame, see the foregoing directions given for "Swing and Climbing Bars."

For the swing, rings, and trapeze, these materials are required:

Rope: Waterproof manila rope, ¾" in diameter (length depending upon height of child; approximately 25' will be needed for swing, 15' for rings, and 15' for trapeze).

Swing seat: 1 piece of 1¼x8 maple or birch,

Trapeze: 1 straight-grained maple, birch, or hickory bar, 1¼" diameter, 24" long.

Rings: 2 galvanized steel or aluminum rings, 1" thick, 8" diameter.

To construct the swing, rings, and trapeze, refer to the previously given directions for "Swing and Climbing Bars."

For the horizontal bar, these are the needed materials:

Bar: 1 piece of pipe, 1" in diameter, 6' long.

Bolts: 2 carriage bolts, ¾" in diameter.

See directions previously given for attaching climbing bars to uprights.

It is especially important that this combination of swing, rings, trapeze, and bar be well constructed. Inspect it frequently. The combination is a good piece of apparatus for a large yard. It may be placed across the end of a yard where it will cover a space about 20' long and 18' wide.

Horizontal Ladder

In this piece of equipment the horizontal ladder is supported by two perpendicular ladders. The easiest way to construct it is to buy a 30' ladder, and cut it into three sections or to buy 3 separate ladders.

Set two of the sections in concrete (see directions previously given for the perpendicular ladders) and place the other section across the top of the horizontal ladder. For older children, the horizontal ladder should be firmly bolted to the uprights at both ends. For children under 5, the horizontal ladder can be made adjustable. Cut a groove in the frame at each end of the horizontal ladder, so that the ladder will not slip when one end is placed on a rung of one of the perpendicular ladders and the other end on the ground. Younger children will like to climb on the ladder and swing from the rungs when it is in this position. A play plank for walking or bouncing may be laid on the lower rungs of the perpendicular ladders or placed at an angle from an upper rung and used as a slide. (See description of play plank.)

A 10' ladder may be bought and used as a horizontal ladder.

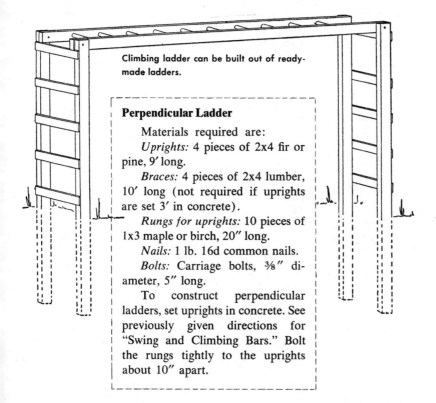

Climbing ladder can be built out of ready-made ladders.

Perpendicular Ladder

Materials required are:

Uprights: 4 pieces of 2x4 fir or pine, 9′ long.

Braces: 4 pieces of 2x4 lumber, 10′ long (not required if uprights are set 3′ in concrete).

Rungs for uprights: 10 pieces of 1x3 maple or birch, 20″ long.

Nails: 1 lb. 16d common nails.

Bolts: Carriage bolts, ⅜″ diameter, 5″ long.

To construct perpendicular ladders, set uprights in concrete. See previously given directions for "Swing and Climbing Bars." Bolt the rungs tightly to the uprights about 10″ apart.

Back-Yard Play Platform

A back yard can be a rocket-launching station, an aircraft carrier or a rodeo corral, depending on the fancy of the youngsters. In summer they shoot down a slide into a plastic wading pool. In winter, their sleds beat Olympic bobsled records on the same steep slope artificially glazed with ice. And the bikes, sleds, toy earth-diggers and other stuff that is always underfoot can be stowed away in a spacious canvas shelter under the deck.

You can build this play platform for considerably less than any comparable outdoor gym you can buy.

The platform—Use a 4′x8′ sheet of exterior plywood as a starting point for measurements. This is to be the platform deck. Four 10′ 4x4's serve for uprights. Creosoted and embedded 24″ in the ground, these are linked with a framework of deck-supporting 2x4's. The long horizontals are nailed to the outside faces of the uprights, with their top surfaces 6′ and 5′ 10″ above the ground, respectively, which gives the deck a rain-shedding pitch. The cross stringers—four of them—measure 3′8″ each. Two are nailed to the inside faces of the uprights.

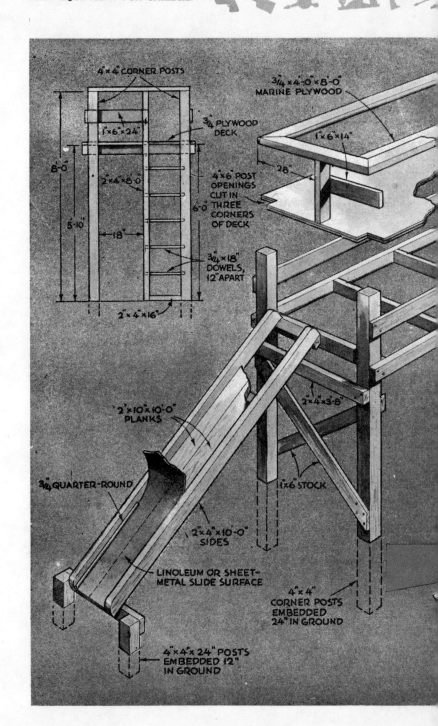

4 x 4 CORNER POSTS

3/4 x 4'-0" x 8'-0" MARINE PLYWOOD

1" x 6" x 24"

3/4 PLYWOOD DECK

1" x 6" x 14"

8'-0"

2" x 4" x 8'-0"

4" x 6" POST OPENINGS CUT IN THREE CORNERS OF DECK

28"

5-10"

6'-0"

18"

3/4" x 18" DOWELS, 12" APART

2" x 4" x 16"

2" x 10" x 10'-0" PLANKS

2" x 4" x 8'-6"

3/4" QUARTER-ROUND

1" x 6" STOCK

2" x 4" x 10'-0" SIDES

LINOLEUM OR SHEET-METAL SLIDE SURFACE

4" x 4" CORNER POSTS EMBEDDED 24" IN GROUND

4" x 4" x 24" POSTS EMBEDDED 12" IN GROUND

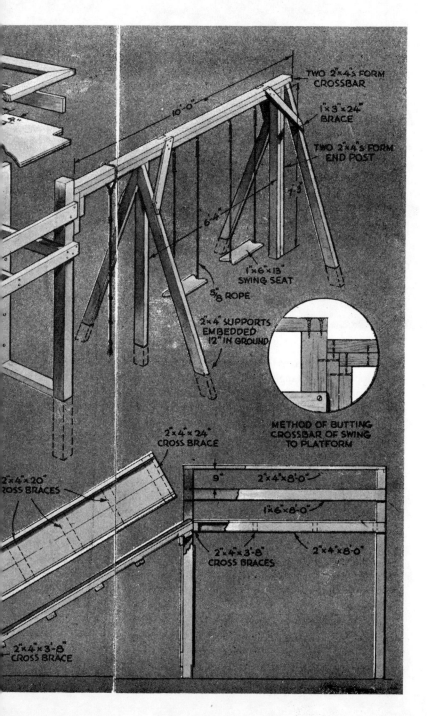

TWO 2"×4's FORM CROSSBAR

1"×3"×24" BRACE

TWO 2"×4's FORM END POST

10'-0"

7'-3"

6'-4"

1"×6"×13" SWING SEAT

5/8 ROPE

2"×4" SUPPORTS EMBEDDED 12" IN GROUND

METHOD OF BUTTING CROSSBAR OF SWING TO PLATFORM

2"×4"×24" CROSS BRACE

2"×4"×20" CROSS BRACES

9"

2"×4"×8'-0"

1"×6"×8'-0"

2"×4"×3'-8" CROSS BRACES

2"×4"×8'-0"

2"×4"×3'-8" CROSS BRACE

The other two are used as intermediate supports. Rectangles 4"x6" sawed from three corners of the plywood sheet, and a 4"x24" rectangle cut from the fourth corner, allow the plywood to be slipped down between the uprights. The 18" recess left on one side of the deck gives a clearway for a ladder.

The ladder—The corner upright on one side of the clearway forms one side of the ladder. The other is 8" of 2x4. The rungs are 18" lengths of ¾" hardwood doweling placed in holes 1" deep at 12" intervals. A spacer block, made of a 2x4, anchors the bottom end of the ladder. A few nails fasten the top to the platform-supporting cross stringer.

Slide support and guardrails— At the other end of the platform, a 3'8" length of 2x4 is nailed to the outside faces of the corner posts, with its top surface 5'6" above the ground. This forms a horizontal support for a slide. Diagonal braces of 1x6" stock are also nailed across the uprights to stiffen the whole assembly. The sections of the uprights projecting above the deck serve as corner posts for a protective fence around the platform. The top guardrails are 2x4's placed flat. Midway between them and the deck there is a seco nd set of rails, broken at the ends to let young gymnasts reach the deck from the ladder and take off on the slide.

Building the slide—Our slide is made of two 2x10 planks, 10' long, cleated side by side to five 2x4 crosspieces. The top crosspiece is beveled and nailed flush against the deck-supporting stringer.

An alternate way of anchoring it would be to use a wider crosspiece, one that would look over the slide support instead of simply resting on it. Either way, the slide is prevented from pulling away from the platform because its bottom crosspiece butts against a 3'8" piece of 2x4 nailed between two 24" lengths of 4x4, each embedded 12" in the ground. Slide sides are 2x4's, nailed to the edges of the planks. For a smooth slide surface linoleum may be used. Sliders are kept from catching their clothes on the nails that hold the linoleum in place along the edges by two strips of quarter-round.

The swing gantry—If 2x4's are nailed together to provide inter-supported ends (see detail drawing),

they make a sturdy swing gantry. The horizontal member is butted to one platform upright, where blocks below it hold it firmly. Three feet out, a single 2x4 separates the climbing rope from the swing section. Both the 2x4 and the built-up 4x4 at the outer end of the gantry are braced by diagonals. Piping may be used for these braces, but 2x4's would do. In either case, both uprights and diagonals should be embedded 12" in the ground. Less than 50' of rope, five screw eyes and two swing seats will round out the project, except for the addition of canvas flaps.

Doll's See-Saw

The doll family can have its own

This shelter for bikes and toys is made by battening canvas flaps to the platform.

When not in use, canvas is rolled and held to the deck with short lashings.

seesaw at the cost of an hour's work and some scrap lumber. For this one, the rockers were jigsawed from ¾" plywood, the seats from ¼"

plywood. A 3" length of scrap about ¾" square braces the rockers. The pieces are assembled with light nails.

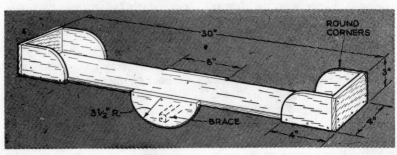

Plans for a doll see-saw.

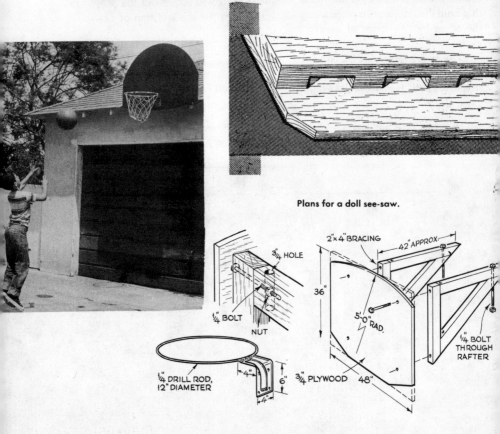

Basketball unit over a garage.

Sand box with awning.

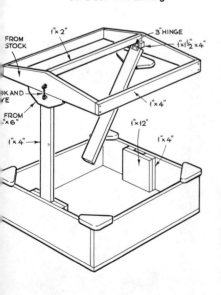

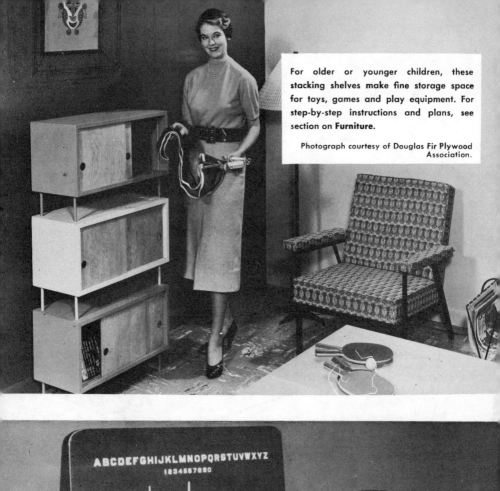

For older or younger children, these stacking shelves make fine storage space for toys, games and play equipment. For step-by-step instructions and plans, see section on **Furniture**.

Photograph courtesy of Douglas Fir Plywood Association.

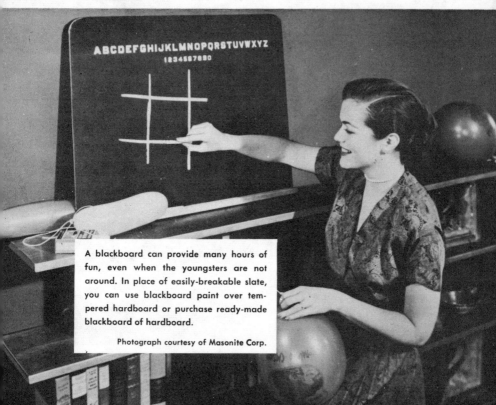

A blackboard can provide many hours of fun, even when the youngsters are not around. In place of easily-breakable slate, you can use blackboard paint over tempered hardboard or purchase ready-made blackboard of hardboard.

Photograph courtesy of Masonite Corp.

Pliers

There are many types of pliers. The following are the most frequently used:

Combination Pliers

The slip joint permits the jaws to be opened wider at the hinge for gripping large diameters. Combination pliers come in sizes from 5" to 10". This is a measure of their overall length.

It's a good idea to have 5" or 6" pliers for light work and 10" pliers for heavy work. The better grades of combination pliers are drop forged steel and withstand hard usage.

These adjustable combination pliers are used principally for holding and bending flat or round stock. The various lengths and shapes of flatnose, roundnose, and half-roundnose pliers make it possible to bend or form metal into a variety of shapes. Many special-purpose pliers are available for specific jobs.

Avoid using pliers on a hardened surface as this dulls the teeth and causes pliers to lose their grip.

Beginners oftentimes use pliers for loosening or tightening nuts. Pliers damage the "flats" of the nut. Use wrenches on nuts—never pliers.

Diagonal Pliers

Other pliers which are useful are the diagonal cutting pliers, usually referred to as diagonals. The diagon-

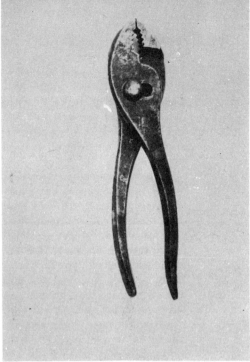

Combination pliers.

Diagonal pliers.

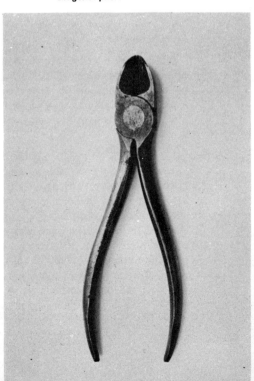

al is a short-jawed cutter with blades at a slight angle. You can use this tool to cut soft wire, and will find that it is practically indispensable in removing or applying safety wire.

Diagonal cutters have been used for a great many purposes for which they were not designed. They have been used to cut insulation from electrical cables, to cut plywood, and to serve as tin snips. They are sturdy tools and will give long service if they are not used for jobs that will damage the cutting edges. Don't cut spring steel wire or hard rivets with them. When you are cutting the largest material within the capacity of a diagonal, use the back of the jaw and not the point. This reduces the tendency to spring the jaws. Once the jaws are sprung it is difficult, if not impossible, to cut fine wire.

Long Nose Pliers

Long nose pliers, either the flat nose or duck bill type, will help you out of such tight spots as recovering a washer or a nut which gets into a place where it is hard to reach.

Electrician's Pliers

Also known as side-cutting pliers, these pliers are practically a must in every handyman's tool chest. Although used extensively in electrical work—cutting and stripping of wires—these pliers are also used for cutting small wires or rods made of brass, copper, aluminum, soft steel and other soft metals. A pair of 6″ or 8″ electrician's pliers, especially those with insulated

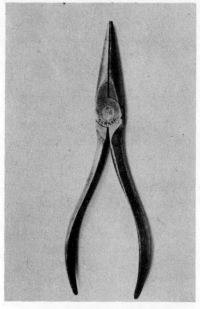

Long nose pliers.

Electrician's pliers.

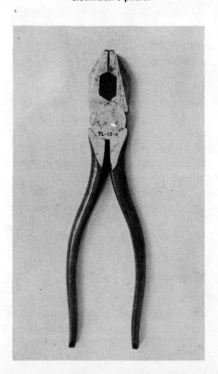

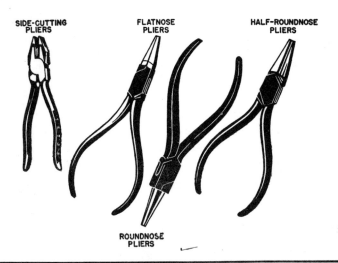

SIDE-CUTTING
PLIERS

FLATNOSE
PLIERS

HALF-ROUNDNOSE
PLIERS

ROUNDNOSE
PLIERS

First Aid for Pliers

AILMENT	REMEDY
Badly rusted	Soak in kerosene for at least 24 hours; then clean with steel wool. Use penetrating oil to work the joint loose. Dry and polish with oil.
Loose jaws or rivet	Close jaws of the pliers and set with broached side* on anvil or metal block. Hit top half of the rivet with flat head of a ball pein hammer.
Tight jaws or rivets	Open pliers to first tight spot and set with broach side down over a hole in a metal block. Hit the rivet squarely with the flat head of a ball pein hammer.
Dull, won't grip	Stroke a checking file across the inside of the jaws, particularly of a long nose pliers.
Dull cutting edge	Place pliers open in a vise with the head flat. Use an India stone to stone out the imperfections and then sharpen with the India stone.

* The rivet through the pliers has two sides—one is round and the other is broached; that is, somewhat star-shaped, a circle with four points.

handles, are well suited for a tool chest.

Parrot-Head Pliers

These adjustable pliers can be used to grip and hold small objects or adjusted like the combination pliers to hold large items. They are particularly useful in automobile work and plumbing.

When adding this useful pair of pliers to a tool chest, it is best to get a larger size first and add a smaller one at a future date. Buy a 12″ or 14″ model first and afterwards you can add and 8″ or 10″ pair of pliers.

Parrot-head pliers.

Vise-grip pliers.

Vise-Grip Pliers

Vise-grip pliers do the job that their name implies. They hold onto any object with a vise-like grip. Most models are adjustable for size and can be used to hold any work since the lower jaw of the pliers is on a swivel so that both jaws can remain parallel to each other and can grip flat stock. The teeth of the jaws enable the pliers to hold on to circular stock as well.

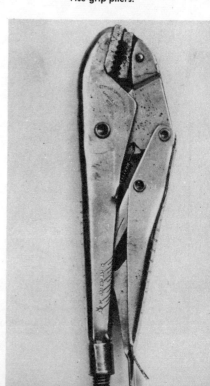

Parallel-Jaw Pliers

The jaws of this type of pliers remain parallel to each other no matter how open or closed the tool is set. The parallel jaw pliers can be used to grip nuts and bolt heads for tightening. Some models come with cutting edge on one side. Because of their leverage, the cutting side jaws will go through an 8d nail with ease.

Furthermore, because of their leverage, these pliers can be used in place of a vise to hold flat objects.

Maintenance

Pliers should be kept clean. Every now and then, wash off the dirt and grit and put a drop of oil on the joint pin. Simple precautions like these will cut down wear and prevent rusting.

Parallel-jaw pliers.

Plough

A plough (or plow) is a groove or a dado cut along the grain of the wood on the face of a board; also, sometimes, a plane used for cutting such grooves.

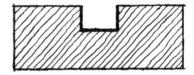

A plough cut in wood.

Plug

This is a plumbing fitting with a threaded end on one side and a square or octagonal head on the other. It is used to close an end of a pipe with a female thread.

This term is also used to describe an electrical unit used to connect a wire into a receptacle. See *Electrical Wiring*.

A plug seals an end of a pipe.

Plumb Bob

A plumb bob is used to check vertical alignment, performing the same job as a spirit level with a vertical guide. Plumb bobs are made of metal with the bottom end coming to a top-like point.

To use a plumb bob, it is best to run a string through the bob and hook the string on a nail where you wish to draw a vertical guide line or check the vertical alignment of an object. The string should be long enough so that the plumb bob is only an inch or two off the floor. Let the cord come to rest; and the line indicated by the string from the nail at top to the bob at the bottom is a perfect vertical line. This technique is used for a starting guide line when hanging wallpaper, setting wall tiles or installing plywood or wood board walls.

A plumb bob is used to obtain a vertical guide line.

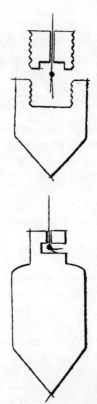

Here are several ways to tie a cord to a plumb bob; it is necessary to tie correctly so that the bob hangs perfectly plumb with point toward the ground in straight line with cord.

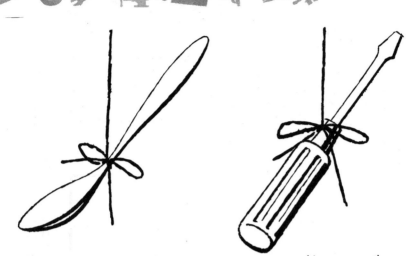

If you don't have a plumb bob, you can use a spoon or screwdriver or any other weight as a substitute to obtain a plumb line.

A plumb line is used to make certain that wallpaper is hung perfectly vertical.

Use a plumb line to check if a stud is properly placed and is perfectly upright.

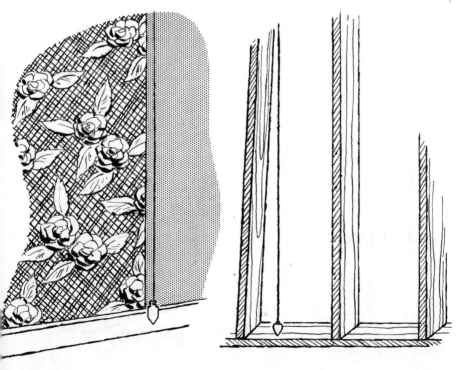

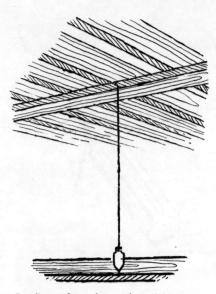

To align a floor plate under a joist overhead, use a plumb line.

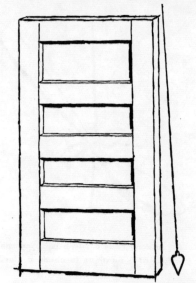

To check if doors are sagging, attach a plumb bob to a line.

A sagging column is easily aligned if you use a plumb line.

Always check a brick wall as you lay it to see if it's perfectly plumb.

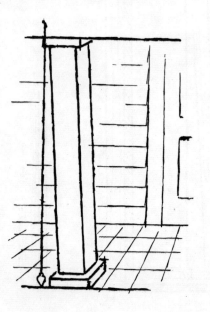

Plumbing

Since plumbing covers a wide area, and the subject is discussed in its various phases throughout these volumes, refer to the sections named in the following classifications for the additional information you need for your plumbing chores:

Bathroom Planning—This section discusses the general plumbing, the location of waste pipes, traps and vent pipe, and fixture installations.

Drainage System—Here you will find detailed information on traps, how to prevent and cure any stoppage; the use of the plumber's friend, chemical cleaners, and other methods to clean out the clogged trap; repair and care of the water closet, flush tank and flush valve.

Faucets—Description of the compression, Fuller ball, and ground-key faucets, and the way to install and repair them, is given in this section. How to eliminate noise in faucet is also explained.

Frozen Pipes—The way to prevent freezing through pipe insulation is included in this section, as well as how to lay underground pipes, and thaw out frozen pipes and drains.

Heating Systems—The operation, maintenance, and repair of the different types of heating systems are explained in these sections. Also included is the way to insulate the pipes, boilers, and ducts in heating systems, as well as the insulation of hot-water tanks. The different heating fuels and methods are explained: coal, oil, gas, etc.

Plastic Pipe—Extruded poly-

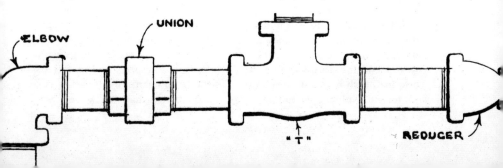

ELBOW   UNION   "T"   REDUCER

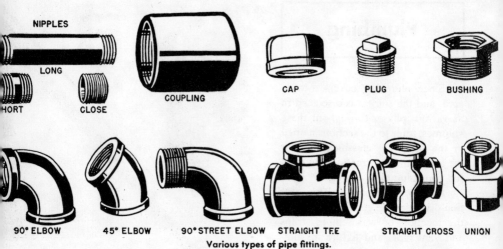

Various types of pipe fittings.

ethylene and vinyl pipe is available for the home handyman. This pipe is easy to work with and all you need to join the pieces together is a screwdriver and adhesive. Plastic pipe is particularly adaptable for exterior use for its does not have to be drained because of the danger of freezing during cold weather.

Pipe Fittings—To connect different sections of pipes, to make iron pipes turn corners and to join two pipes of different diameters, it is necessary to use a pipe fitting.

Valves—Whereas faucets control the flow of water at the end of a pipe, a valve controls the flow of water between pipes. See this section for details about the different types of valves.

Water, Shutting Off—For information on the shut-off methods to control or stop the flow of water to the house, see this section.

Plumbing— Basic Data

In this section, you will find the basic information about pipes and plumbing. In the following sections you will find the details on how to work, first, with brass and iron pipe and, second, with copper tubing.

Types of Pipe

Black iron pipe is not suitable to carry water in either the supply or drainage systems for it rusts too quickly and will cause stoppages in a relatively short period of time.

Galvanized pipe is the standard type used for home supply and drainage lines because of its comparatively low price and its fair resistance to corrosion. It resists corrosion better than black iron pipe but rates poorly when compared with brass or copper.

Cast iron pipe is used primarily for drainage systems. See section on *Cast Iron Pipe* for how-to-details.

Brass pipe offers the advantages of iron pipe plus the fact that it does not rust. Furthermore, because of its smoother interior wall section, it offers less resistance to the flow of water. It has, therefore, replaced galvanized iron pipe in many homes equipped with "better" plumbing.

Tools To Do the Job

While it is impractical to buy all the tools needed for every type of home improvement and repair, there are certain specialized tools which the homeowner should add to his tool collection. Some of the other, more expensive and specialized tools, can be rented from hardware stores. However, if you do extensive plumbing—either repairs or improvements—it may be wise to purchase some of the equipment you might normally rent.

1. A vise for holding the pipe while it is being cut is absolutely necessary when working with brass or iron pipe. It is unimportant if you use copper tubing. You can get a pipe vise or use pipe jaws in a regular vise.

2. Pipe cutters make it easier to cut pipe; they are faster than a hacksaw and produce a better job—the end of the pipe is cut perfectly flush. This square cut is particularly important when it is necessary to thread brass or iron pipe or flare copper tubing for solderless connectors.

A bibb seat dresser is used to smooth the worn surface of a faucet seat to prevent the chewed-up metal from eating away the washer.

Pipe jaws in a machinist's vise holds the pipe with head stock and a die cutter is used to thread the iron or brass pipe.

3. Pipe reamer is used to remove the internal burrs resulting from cutting. Reamers come in different diameters, adjustable for several sizes of pipe. They are used with a brace. For copper tubing, however, the better pipe cutters have a reamer attached.

4. Pipe dies are used to thread the end of brass or iron pipe. They come in sets, normally, together with a handle.

5. Pipe taps are used to make internal threads. The size of the tap is normally marked on the shank. In using the accompanying table the suggested tap size is recommended for the nominal diameter of the pipe and not its actual diameter. See *Dies and Taps* for additional information. Here, however, are tap drill sizes for American National Pipe Threads:

A hacksaw can be used to cut brass or iron pipe as well as copper tubing.

This is one type of a flaring tool. The nut end of the fitting is placed over the pipe and the flaring tool inserted into the open tubing. A few taps with the hammer will flare the end of the tubing.

Nominal size of the pipe	Threads per inch	Tap Size
⅛″	27	$11/_{32}$″
¼″	18	$7/_{16}$″
⅜″	18	$37/_{64}$″
½″	14	$23/_{32}$″
¾″	14	$59/_{64}$″
1 ″	11½	1 $5/_{32}$″
1¼″	11½	1 ½ ″
1½″	11½	$147/_{64}$″
2 ″	11½	2 $7/_{32}$″

6. Pipe wrenches vary depending upon their purpose. Wrenches used with pipe must have jaws that will grip the round exterior surface securely. Normally, Stillson wrenches are used for the job, but it is also possible to use a strap wrench (a belt is used in place of the jaws) or a pipe tongs (a link chain is used in place of the jaws).

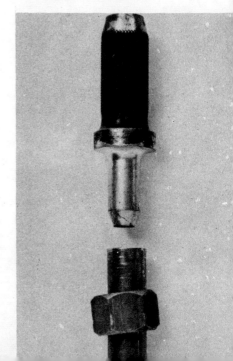

The hexagonal fittings of solderless connectors, tops of valves and faucets, and other non-round surfaces require the use of other types of wrenches. A monkey or open-end wrench is best for these uses. A parrot-head pliers can be used if the surface is protected by tape to prevent the plier's teeth from "chewing" into the metal.

For additional details about which size wrench to use, see the table under "Pipe Fittings" in the section: *Plumbing—Working with Brass and Iron Pipe.*

7. Hacksaw can be used for cutting pipe or tubing. Set the blade in the frame so that the teeth point forward because the cutting is done only on the forward stroke.

• For iron and brass pipe, use a saw blade with 24 teeth per inch.

• For conduit and thin tubing, use a blade with 32 teeth per inch.

8. A blow torch is necessary when working with cast iron pipe as well as soldered fittings with copper tubing. This can be the gasoline pump type or the pressurized-fuel, disposable can type.

9. Tube benders are used with soft copper tubing. With the tube bender or bending spring, the tube can then be bent to any angle without collapsing the walls of the tube. Tube benders usually come in kits but individual sizes can be purchased.

10. Flaring tool is used with solderless connectors and copper tubing. There are two types available. One is a tapered unit which is inserted into the tubing and the outside end hit with a hammer to flare the pipe. The other is a yoke unit

This is another type of flaring tool. The tubing is set into the proper opening and clamped in place. It is then flared by turning the handle which depresses the flaring end of the yoke unit.

Taps are used to cut internal threads in pipe.

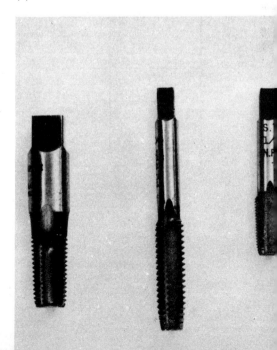

which is adjustable for copper tubing of varying diameters.

11. Plunger or plumber's friend is used to remove obstructions in a pipe by air pressure. See *Plunger* and *Drainage Systems*.

12. Closet auger or "snake" is used to remove obstructions within a pipe by physical means. The metal spring steel or coiled wire is pushed through the pipe to clean it out.

13. Bibb seat dresser is used to resurface the seat of a faucet or compression valve.

Pipe Measurements

When making a new installation or a repair, it is necessary to measure the pipe accurately. This is important whether you order the pipe and have it cut to size and threaded by a professional or you cut and thread the pipe yourself.

The easiest way to measure pipe, if a professional will cut and thread it, is to draw the exact pipe diagram and then mark the measurements. The professional can figure out the exact size of each piece.

The accompanying tables and diagrams should help you make an exact dimension drawing or determine the sizes yourself.

PIPE FITTING DISTANCE	
Size of Pipe	Distance Pipe is Screwed into Fitting (A in Sketch)
$\frac{1}{8}$"	$\frac{1}{4}$"
$\frac{1}{4}$"	$\frac{3}{8}$"
$\frac{3}{8}$"	$\frac{3}{8}$"
$\frac{1}{2}$"	$\frac{1}{2}$"
$\frac{3}{4}$"	$\frac{1}{2}$"
1 "	$\frac{9}{16}$"
$1\frac{1}{4}$"	$\frac{5}{8}$"
$1\frac{1}{2}$"	$\frac{5}{8}$"
2 "	$\frac{11}{16}$"

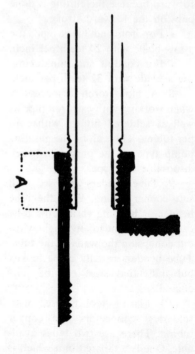

Fitting distance, that is, the distance that a pipe will screw into a fitting, valve or faucet, depends upon the diameter of the pipe. See the accompanying table for exact details.

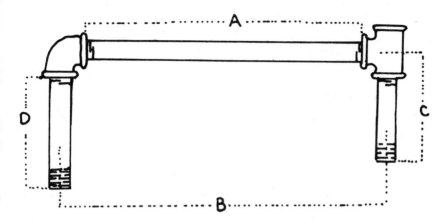

Methods of measuring pipe—A is a face-to-face measurement but it does not take into account the additional piece of the pipe that goes into the fitting; use the fitting table to obtain the exact size of the pipe; B is a center-to-center measurement; C is a center-to-end measurement; D is an end-to-face measurement; add the part that fits into the fitting and you have the exact length of the pipe.

Pipes have to be measured and cut exactly to prevent leaks in the system. It is important to determine the distance from the end of a pipe to the center of the fitting; that is, distance X in the sketch. This varies depending upon the diameter of the pipe as noted in the accompanying table.

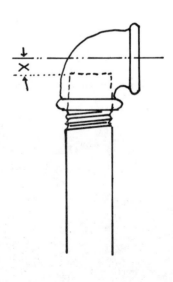

DISTANCE FROM END OF PIPE TO CENTER OF FITTING	
Size of Pipe	Dimension X*
½"	⅝"
¾"	13/16"
1 "	⅞"
1¼"	1⅛"
1½"	1 5/16"
2 "	1 3/16"

* This applies to 90° elbow, Street L and T's.

Plumbing— Working with Brass and Iron Pipe

You can cut brass or iron pipe with an ordinary hand hacksaw, a power hacksaw, or a pipe cutter. You'll prefer to use the pipe cutter for the average job, but the power hacksaw is faster if you have a large number of pieces to cut or if the pipe has a thick wall. The pipe cutter has a special alloy steel cutting wheel and two pressure rollers. These are adjusted and tightened by turning the handle. The whole tool is revolved around the pipe.

The operation of the pipe cutter leaves a shoulder on the outside of the pipe and a burr on the inside. Always remove that inside burr or the ragged edges will catch dirt and other solid matter, and will block the flow. The burring reamer is the tool you use to remove the burr.

Pipe Threading

Pipe fittings have tapered threads and require special dies, called pipe dies, so they can be turned up tight and leakproof. A stock is used to turn the dies, and the same stock can be used for threading several sizes of pipe. Most pipe dies can be adjusted to cut

How To Cut and Thread Iron Pipe

1. Pipe can be cut in a pipe vise or in a machinist's vise equipped with special pipe jaws.

2. After a piece of pipe has been cut to the required size, any inside burrs are removed with a reamer. The outside burr can be removed with a file.

slightly different depths of thread so that a longer or shorter thread on the end of the pipe can be obtained as desired. To cut the threads, secure the work and hold the stock; then proceed as when using any other die; keep the work well oiled. It is a good idea to test the thread with a standard pipe fitting when the operation is finished.

Pipe Assembly

Threaded water pipe joints are usually made up with red lead as a seal. Steam pipe threads are sealed with graphite paint. Put the sealing compound on the pipe threads only —so it won't get inside the pipe and form a dangerous obstruction. Make sure the threads are clean before you apply the sealing compound.

Threaded joints should be screwed together by hand and tightened with a pipe wrench—commonly called a "Stillson." The pipe should be held in a pipe vise during assembly, but if it's impossible to use a vise the pipe may be held with another pipe wrench.

How tight should you tighten a joint? Experience is the best teacher. Usually you will have two or three unused threads on a properly cut pipe thread. If all the threads are used, the wedging action of the tapered thread may cause the fitting to split.

Pipe wrenches are made in a number of sizes (lengths). Use the following table as a guide for selecting the best size to use:

Wrench Size	for	Pipe Size (in inches)
6		¼
10		⅜ and ½
14		¾
18		1 and 1¼
24		1½ and 2

Size of Brass and Iron Pipe

Nominal Size	Inside Diameter	Outside Diameter
⅛	¼	⅜
¼	⅜	$17\frac{}{32}$
⅜	½	$11\frac{}{16}$
½	⅝	$13\frac{}{16}$
¾	$13\frac{}{10}$	1
1	$1\frac{1}{16}$	$1\frac{5}{16}$
1¼	1⅜	1⅝
1½	1⅝	1⅞
2	$2\frac{1}{16}$	2⅜
2½	$2\frac{9}{16}$	2⅞
3	$3\frac{1}{16}$	3½
3½	$3\frac{9}{16}$	4
4	4	4½

3. You can thread your own pipe or have the hardware dealer do the job for you. Thread-cutting die equipment can be rented for a nominal amount if you wish to do the job yourself. All you have to do is set the die stock in place and start turning it on the pipe. While threading the pipe, apply liberal doses of pipe cutting oil. This makes the job easier and results in less wear-and-tear on the die head.

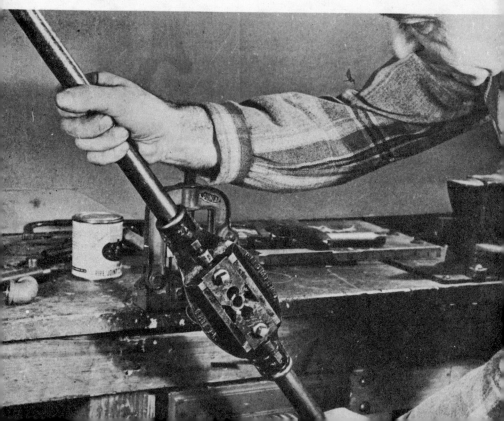

4. To prevent possible leaks when attacking fittings, wind lampwick clockwise around the threaded end of the pipe. Then, to make the joint perfectly waterproof, coat the pipe and lampwick with joint compound. This should be done to all male pipe connections.

5. Where it is possible, attach the fittings while the pipe is in the vise. Turn the two parts together and continue until the right amount of the male threaded section is inside the fitting. (See table on fitting distances.) With a cloth, wipe off the excess joint compound.

6. If the pieces have to be put together without the aid of a vise, then two wrenches are needed for the job. One wrench is used to hold the installed pipe steadily in place and the other is used to turn on the fitting. Remember, you turn clockwise to tighten, counter-clockwise to loosen the pipes.

Plumbing— Working with Copper Tubing

Adding plumbing for a new bathroom, piping a cellar tub or darkroom sink, or running underground lines to outdoor pools or sprinkling systems are weekend projects, requiring only a hacksaw to make a few cuts and a small torch to solder connections together.

There's no need for the Stillsons, threading dies, or pipe vises that you need for galvanized-steel plumbing. In many cases, you can use simple screw-together fittings that eliminate even the job of soldering.

Types of Tubing

Enormous presses cold-extrude seamless copper tubing from solid billets of the pure metal. The tubing comes from the die work-hardened, and some of it is then annealed to soften it.

You can snake this easily bent, soft-tempered tubing down through

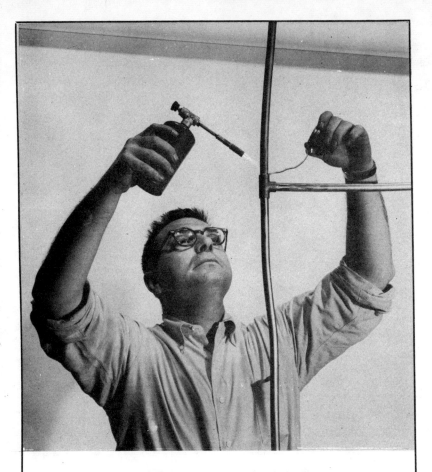

10 Ways to Improve Your Home Plumbing with Copper Tubing

1. Extend a branch water line to supply an added-on bathroom.

2. Replace old radiators with modern baseboard or radiant wall units.

3. Run an underground water line to a garage or other outbuildings.

4. Replace rusted and lime-clogged water lines where pressure has dropped.

5. Install a sink in a basement darkroom or playroom bar.

6. Run a fuel line from an outdoor oil tank (but not gas without an expert).

7. Install a permanent sprinkling system for your lawn.

8. Mount a shower head over a bathtub that doesn't already have one.

9. Put in extra sill cocks around your foundation for garden hoses.

10. Pipe underground water to a garden pool, fountain, or bird bath.

Thread it through—You can easily string soft-tempered, flexible tubing through holes in floor joists or wall studs. Straight hard-temper sections can be notched into edges of beams if code permits, or nailed to face with small pipe straps. Make bends gentle to ease water flow, avoid strain at sharp corners. Soaping outside of pipe first helps you slide it through holes.

walls and through holes bored in studs and joists just like electrical wiring. When you come to a corner, you simply bend it where you want it to go, saving the installation of an angle fitting. Because it comes in lengths up to 100′, you can make long, unbroken runs that virtually eliminate all connections except at the ends.

Outdoors, the flexible soft tubing withstands an occasional accidental freeze without bursting. When run underground, it "gives" as the earth settles and heaves, minimizing breakage. It also is less subject to damage from expansion and contraction, which in hotwater lines is as much as 1¼″ per 100′.

Hard-temper tubing, not annealed, comes in standard 20′ lengths. Use this rigid tube if you're a stickler for neatness and also in places where exposed lines may be kicked, knocked or otherwise damaged.

Hard tubing can be bent, but only in a leverage-type tube bender. If one isn't available, it's best to

Cut off the end—In tight spots where you can't saw tubing, use this roller-type cutter that's simply clamped to pipe, then twisted around it. Cutter leaves heavy burr on inside edge that must be reamed out before attaching fittings.

Saw it to length—Simple miter box made of wood scraps insures square cuts. Space sides of box apart same width as tubing (¾" spacer for ½" pipe; 1" for ¾" pipe) to hold it snugly during sawing. Use 32-tooth hacksaw blade.

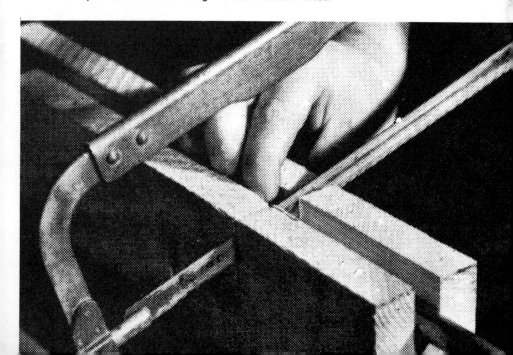

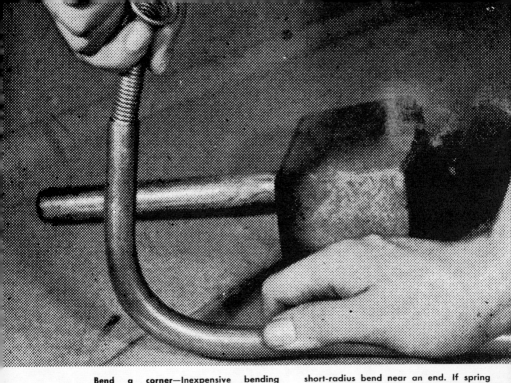

Bend a corner—Inexpensive bending spring, inserted in tubing, keeps walls from collapsing when you have to make a short-radius bend near an end. If spring sticks inside, tap tubing with a mallet to jar it loose for easy removal.

Hook it up—To join copper pipe to regular galvanized-steel plumbing, use an adapter fitting that has standard pipe threads on one end and copper joint on other. Fittings come with flare or solder joints and male or female threads.

figure on using the standard angle fittings, which probably won't take any longer to solder on than it would to make bends. If you have a lot of corners to turn, you can always insert a length of soft tubing, making the bends in it, even where the rest of the plumbing is of the rigid type.

Pick the Right Weight

Both hard and soft tubing come in two different weights, called K and L, that are commonly used in home plumbing:

Type K, a thick-walled, heavy-duty tubing, is best for exposed lines that might become dented and is only a little more expensive than the lighter weight. It's also used for underground lines that are subject to strain, for gas service lines, and for the very best plumbing and heating systems.

Type L is a lighter weight that's used for most home-plumbing and radiant-heating work. It's fine for all average indoor lines that are reasonably well protected.

What Size To Use

If you buy small-size tubing at an auto-supply store for your car, you'll find it sold according to its outside diameter. In all other cases, though, copper tubing is classified according to its nominal inside diameter, just as steel pipe is, and this is what you ask for at plumbing shops.

For homes with normal water pressure, use a ¾″ copper branch line if it supplies two or more fixtures; ⅝″ tubing to sill cocks; ½″

1. To make strong joint, copper must be thoroughly clean. Rub outside of tubing and inside of fitting with fine abrasive cloth. Remove burrs inside pipe with a round file.

How To Make a Soldered Connection

2. Apply thin coat of non-corrosive soldering flux to outside of tubing and inside of fitting. Then slip the tube into the fitting and wipe off excess flux around the joint.

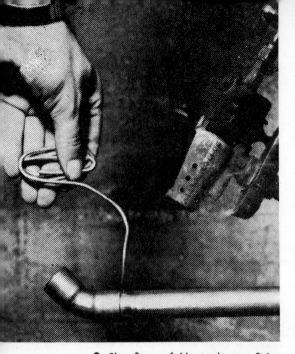

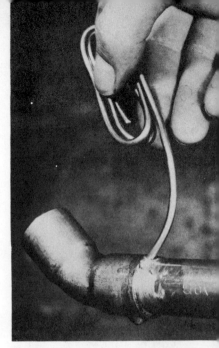

3. Play flame of blowtorch over fitting and tubing to heat both evenly. When copper is hot enough, solder flows freely when you touch joint. Capillary action draws solder in.

4. Keep feeding solder into joint, removing the blowtorch each time solder is applied. The connection is complete when a bright ring of molten solder shows all around the joint.

tubing to individual bathroom or kitchen fixtures. As a rule of thumb, it's safe to use tubing one size smaller than the galvanized pipe you'd otherwise put in.

5. Brush off excess solder with old paintbrush. This will also show if solder has completely filled joint. If not, add more. Don't move joint until solder has become cool and hard.

Fittings Make It Easy

Two types of connectors give you a choice of soldering or not. A soldered-on fitting can be used on both hard and soft tubing, while the solderless kind, called a flare fitting, is recommended only for the soft.

Use the solder joint for neat, permanent jobs. Flare fittings are more expensive, but are good for temporary lines or installations that may have to be disassembled since they are easily taken apart and re-used. They may also be a lifesaver in tight spots where the use of a blowtorch for soldering might be

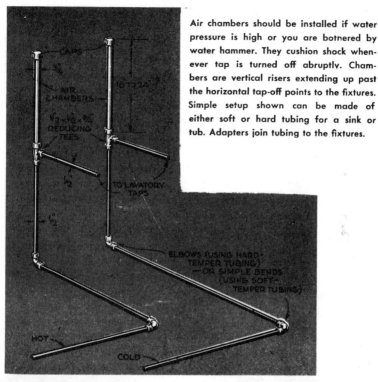

Air chambers should be installed if water pressure is high or you are bothered by water hammer. They cushion shock whenever tap is turned off abruptly. Chambers are vertical risers extending up past the horizontal tap-off points to the fixtures. Simple setup shown can be made of either soft or hard tubing for a sink or tub. Adapters join tubing to the fixtures.

difficult or dangerous.

Both types come in a complete line of Ts, elbows, couplings, reducers, valves, sill cocks and other fittings. You can also buy combination fittings that have standard pipe threads on one end and either a flare or solder connection on the other.

Installation

Whenever possible, keep cold- and hot-water lines at least 6″ apart to reduce sweating. If you are providing for an automatic washer or if water pressure is high, it's a good idea to put in air chambers at fixtures to cushion water hammer— the noisy shock when a tap is turned off suddenly. A sketch shows how this is easily done.

Install all horizontal water lines with a slight pitch, about ¼″ per foot, to allow complete draining when necessary. Soft tubing should be supported by straps every 6′ to prevent sagging, hard tubing every 10′ or at most 12′.

If you're burying an underground line, don't put a cindeer fill in the trench. When the ground becomes wet, sulfur compounds in the cinders will corrode the tubing.

When you're tapping into existing plumbing, especially for hot water, make sure it's one of the domestic lines and not part of the heating system—often an easy mistake to make. Trace the lines carefully back so you are sure where

they come from. Besides shutting off the main water supply, close off any intermediate valves that will reduce the amount of water that will drain from a cut line.

There's another good thing about copper tubing. While it's slightly more expensive than steel pipe, it can't rust or clog and if properly treated will last indefinitely.

Incorrect flaring of copper tubing will cause a solderless connector to leak. Here are three examples of improper flaring.

FLARE TOO SHORT

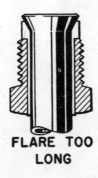

FLARE TOO LONG

FLARE NOT STRAIGHT

How To Make a Flared Connection

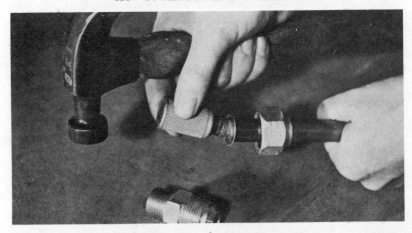

1. Solderless joint requires two-part fitting that clamps tubing in between. To make flare, slip sleeve nut on pipe first, then hammer flaring tool into end to roll edges outward.

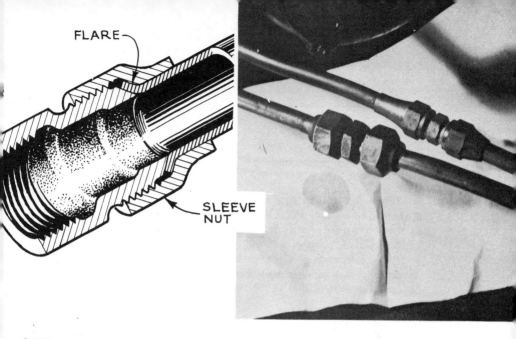

FLARE

SLEEVE NUT

2. When sleeve nut is slipped up against flare and screwed to other half of fitting, the two parts squeeze the tubing tightly between them. Such joints withstand 3,000 lb. per sq. in.

3. After joints are made, be sure to check for any slow leaks. Slide sheet of paper under joints and leave overnight. Any drippings will show up as spots on the paper.

4. Flare fittings make it easy to disconnect lines on equipment that must be disassembled from time to time, like this oilburner unit. Draw nuts up tight, but don't twist joints.

5. You can fix your car, too, with S.A.E. flare couplings that fit automotive parts. Using soft tubing, you can replace fuel and other lines that have become worn or broken.

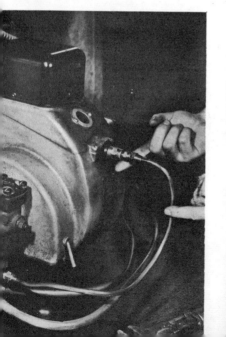

Plunger

This is the familiar suction cup at the end of a stick, which is used to open up clogged waste lines. It is known as the "plumber's friend," and more information is given on its use under that item in the section on *Drainage System*.

That old stand-by, the "plumber's friend," is used to clear clogged pipes.

This specialized plunger acts like a pump. The rubber end is set into the sink opening and the air plus water forces the pipe open.

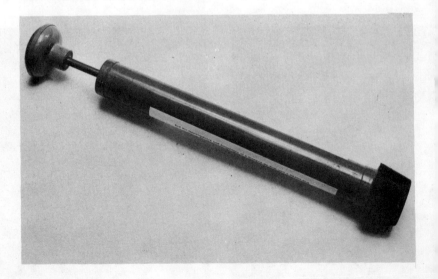